Faith is King in Love and Kindness

CHINITA OLIVIÁ DUKES

authorHOUSE

AuthorHouse™
1663 Liberty Drive
Bloomington, IN 47403
www.authorhouse.com
Phone: 833-262-8899

Published by AuthorHouse   02/01/2023

ISBN: 978-1-6655-5597-5 (sc)
ISBN: 978-1-6655-5596-8 (e)

Library of Congress Control Number: 2022905633

Print information available on the last page.

Scripture quotations marked KJV are from the Holy Bible, King James Version
(Authorized Version). First published in 1611. Quoted from the KJV Classic
Reference Bible, Copyright © *1983 by The Zondervan Corporation.*

CONTENTS

INTRODUCTION

america is a beautiful country, God's masterpiece, a rainbow nation comprised of many different ethnic cultures. The founding fathers sealed a declaration on July 4, 1776 making America about 246 years old. History tells us that the English ships were one of the first ships to hit the shores and colonized what they named America. A land previously owned by native culture, everyone else came to the shores of America were of Immigrant decent.

Americans has little to no time to waste in repairing a wounded nation, to pull themselves back together and fill the cracks that's breaking America apart. To unify themselves and stand fast honoring past human sacrifices made from America's ancestry to overcome this division. America must live out its realities and connect the dots for seeking a healthier lifestyle.

The world has experienced many disasters resulting from selfish acts against mankind. Today men and women has forgotten how to maintain practical ethical duties along with spiritual duties to maintain healthy living. Many men and women who has reached successful living, has lost their divine spark for human justice because greed has blinded the course towards humanity.

There is something more precious than money, noted in Proverbs 20:15 " There is gold and a multitude of rubies; but the lips of knowledge are a precious jewel." Seeking knowledge for natural and spiritual wellness is an asset for successful living.

America's middle-class workers are the driving force to turning the wheels of this country. Middle class participants are the primary stakeholders feeding the federal and local state agencies with their hard-earned revenue keeping this country in operation, safe and moving forward.

The American people has forgotten what Democracy stands for and find themselves caught in the web of the spider, grabbing on to smoking mirrors, and authorities speaking with false tongues. Setting aside Jesus the one who really loves you, noted in Proverbs 8:7 " I love those who love me, and those who seek me diligently find me" We have to seek and practice the principle of love to get positive results, noted in this scripture, 1 John 4:19 "We love because he loved us"

People who really love America are steadily losing their trust, faith, voices and power in the America's dream. The working-class families are being dismantled with false trues, false promises and hidden sink holes. Elected national and state officials down playing certain communities to stop funding services, but yet those elected officials are responsible for the warfare of communities they represent.

Messages presented in this writing is a national round-up for all mankind to "**Soldier-up**" in building a new Infrastructure necessary to restore and build a better America along with our spirituality supporting the way, noted in Psalms 16:11 "Thou will show me the path of life in thy presence is fullness of joy, at the right hand there are pleasures or evermore" why can't everyone feel the fullness of joy? Remember human beings make the world go around!

Faith is King was written to give you courage to take this spiritual walk to tackle whatever it takes to stay in the right direction and to allow God's help in your dreams. Remember if you want to live the dream, you have to work towards your dreams.

Plant your vision in your mind, apply the vision to accomplish your goals, depend on no one to support your vision, especially when efforts come from the heart. Faith is king can be that force in messaging factual information to take the lead to building a true Christian vision.

Faith is King sets up a wellness agenda for a Biblical diet of scripture nutrition to initiate spiritual growth and understanding holiness, to stimulate the thought process, triggering "**Cognitive Thinking**" which empowers the brain to act, this ideology helps the brain to process information. In return this process should give you guidance and direction in decision making, that gives energy needed to improve healthy living and build a solid personal portfolio for you and your family.

It is also important that these messages be presented through the content and context of narratives through descriptions and explanatory languages. Some messages have actual dialog from Bible scriptures allow you to visualize the similarities attached to natural living. To recognize the truth of the importance of your existence with God today and the need to harmonize your lifestyle with natural and spiritual harmony.

The narratives written provides the reader with realities leading to highways to positive change. Faith leads the way only if you believe in yourself to accomplish strong faith during healthy living. To take the journey for change, knowledge will be your best friend Noted in Proverbs " To know wisdom and Instruction; to perceive the words of understanding" Always remember change takes preparation, you must have the tools to develop a healthy livelihood.

Important pathways to faith introduce exploratory readings focused on facts, references and resources to help give direction towards building personal portfolios, which allows you to create your own masterpiece in healthy living. Knowledge makes you a "**Champion**," bringing honor and service into your journey.

Faith is king looks through the lens of Kerygmatic history, a history that describes the act of preaching to encourage students to encounter the pathways of Jesus Christ, which is centered around structure of truths in a systematic study to directly and immediately serve in preparing and promoting resourceful truths for Christian guidance. In resetting our lives, we need more avenues for the right continuous learning to live a natural life with a spiritual orbit.

In understanding Kerygmatic history orchestrates scientific theology, because we live in a natural world where science plays a major part in problem solving America's solution for living and the window for understanding.

The Covid 19 is a perfect example of utilizing Kerygmatic history because it allows you to look through the lens of science to understand bible scriptures prophecy, that shed lights on today's America's events. America's contributes to Kerygmatic history, when trying to cure an invisible killing epidemic virus, that Biblical history has noted would happen both in the past and present in one's timeline.

Kerygmatic history prepares and promotes holistic teaching used for daily living, including theological systems representing its main focus on positions in God's setting of doctrinal statements and scared scriptures. Kerygmatic history shines a light on religious or moral commandments in the same frame work of God's purpose for daily living.

The scope of theological systems represents positions which contains mythological characteristic to living in a natural world and respecting that spirituality is also a characteristic in our daily living.

Collectively with the right insight of knowledge you can see through the lens of holistic behaviors from Christian maintenance. It is important to nourish a missionary learning to respect the value of Biblical history. It is important to note in Proverb 24:14 " So shall the knowledge of wisdom be unto thy soul, when thou hast found it, then there shall be a reward, and thy expectation shall not be cut off."

Educational networks in natural living, offers a piece of the American pie (American Dream) through pathways of education. Your educational knowledge will determine how big the piece of the American dream you will own. Spirituality's messages are designed to give you an invitation to explore the truth on how to live with a spiritual orbit in a natural setting.

Working with factual knowledge helps explain important words, draw parallels between specific occurrence past and presents. Describe historical and textual content messages that puts a light on passages that shed light on one another. Certain natural and spiritual tools are used as devices to equipped you to stay on course to healthy Living.

The expectations and accountability of all individuals is supported by our society's norms. Society norms have been set in place since ancient times. We live in a society that expects everyone to be self-sufficient, independent and accountable for building their own healthy life style. You are responsible for building and managing your own welfare, therefore everyone needs the necessary tools and skills to maintain that life style.

Nothing is free in America, knowledge is your best friend to be self-maintained, knowing how to stay in charge with continuous learning. Knowledge is the key to being a true Christian, without Christian knowledge your life will have limitations. Noted in Proverbs 18:15 " The heart of the prudent gathers knowledge and the ear of the wise seek knowledge." In America you have to seek out your American dream.

Accepting a **New Day** approach for change, carries important tools to advance thinking, but first you must empower the **Brain,** the greatest asset a person owns to regulate corrective thinking. The brain is like a sponge which can absorb unlimited amount of Information. Igniting the brain sends important messages to your cognitive thinking tool box, signaling for the right decisions. The bottom line to achieving successful performance, is learning how to build and harmonize natural and spiritual living for a healthier life style through corrective thinking.

The times and events you experience in one's life will be similar to past Biblical history. God will not change his doctrine, whatever is needed to navigate one's life, the Bible scriptures has already written principles and guidelines to accomplish the experience. All through past and present Biblical history, men and women have tried to change God's order to benefit themselves, depending on what drives them. The only thing that changes in time for the present generations is modernization and not God's word.

Keeping an open mind during this journey for change, will allow you to experience true realities in making better decisions for your own tailor-made lifestyle. The bottom line to successful living is learning how to build spiritual platforms around natural living.

Before anyone can achieve healthy living, one most look at the entire spectrum of the American experience and events to determine positive pathways for better living. Preparation for change is a solution to healthy living, corrective learning is your benefactor, which is crucial for harmonizing life towards spiritual maturity.

In this world everyone is responsible for carrying their own cross, both naturally and spiritually, why not be prepared Noted in (Tim 4:3-4) "The time will come when they will not endure sound doctrine, but after their own lusts shall they heap to themselves teacher, having itching ears;" Why not depend on self and what is true, people in power will turn away from the cry of the people after being elected. Have these ruthless politicians turned our lives upside down?

GOD'S KINGDOM

Today's fast-tracking world must include God's purpose and plans in conquering the world. No one knows when God's work will be completed noted in Matt 24:36 "But concerning that day and hour no one knows, not even the angels of heaven nor the son, but the father only". You must be faithful until the end of your time. Stepping away from God's theology will bear hot everlasting consequences. Noted in Galatians 6:7 "Be not deceived; God is not mocked; for whatsoever a man soweth that shall he also reap".

God continues to observe behaviors and actions of his people during their timeline, God will judge a person's hearts by the fruits of their labor. It is wise to harmonize your living to include working on one's eternal life, a kingdom ruled by God. Eternal life is important because we live to die so pay attention to Jude 1:21 " Keep yourselves in the love of God, looking for the mercy of our Lord Jesus Christ unto eternal life," when you believe God is God, then you will soldier up to stand in the right lane of life.

God has gone to extreme measures in demonstrating his purpose, noted in James 3:16 "For God so loved the world, that he gave his only forgotten son, that whosoever believeth in him should not perish, but have everlasting life" All you have to do is **believe** you can empower yourself, to be that new creature to build a healthier life style. God promised to keep your mental and physical body healthy to manage and build healthy living if you only **believe!**

There is no other human being in this world who can give you this type of agreement, guarantee, promise of assurance but God, noted in (Rev 21:3)" He will dwell with them and they will be his people, and God himself will be with them as their God"

Looking back at Biblical history reflects human's conduct starting with the existence of Adam and Eve, a great creation. God made a perfect union and added the garden of Eden as a perfect environment for Adam and Eve needs and pleasures. Now let's examine the real messaging and the facts of this situation for the true understanding.

Life began with Adam and Eve where everything from the garden of Eden was given to them. The only restriction in the garden of Eden was the tree of knowledge of good and evil. There was no evil in the garden of Eden until the devil entered as a snake to deceive God's order with his first born. When Adam disobeyed, he restricted his relationship with God by eating the forbidden fruit given to him by Eve.

Bible History gives a self-explanation on how Eve was approached by Satan, disguised as a talking serpent questioning Eve. The serpent asked Eve" Why have you not eaten from the tree standing in the middle of the garden? Eve explained to Satan "That is the tree of knowledge of good and evil "and God said, (Genesis 3:3)" But of the fruit of the tree which is in the midst of the garden, God hath said ye shall not eat of it, neither shall ye touch it, lest ye die. "Adam and Eve was already warned by God.

The devil at his best chose Eve to do his dirty work, to help influence Adam participation in the deviance of God's expectation of Adam. Satan's influence and persuasion convinced Eve to pick the fruit from the tree of knowledge and also gave some to Adam. Adam and Eve had violated God's word which opened up the world to evil behaviors and wickiness.

Now Adam in trouble with God through Eve, who Adam named "Mother of all living," has also violated God's commandment stated in (Genesis 4: 16-17) Image having the opportunity to be in your home, with no responsibilities, knowing all your provision would be taken care of for the rest of your life, if you only had to trust in the "Almighty God" and his instructions.

When Adam and Eve violated God's commandment instructed for both, this activated the meaning of "Tree of Knowledge of Good and Evil.", causing a new revelation, introducing and creating the atmosphere of good and evil, now identified in the world through the acts of Adam and Eve.

Adam and Eve refused to listen causing life to change, listening is a skill, not listening bears consequences. God took back his promise because of Adam and Eve's disobedience. From that day forth, Adam and Eve disobedience caused men and women to work for their living until life ends.

In the beginning of the world, another revelation takes place, on earth men and women spoke only one language, there in a city called Babel, where Gods people dwelled, tried to build a tower to heaven, a land only occupied by God. Noted in the book of Jasper, during this time man ruled the earthly cities with kings and their servants.

The people of Babel worshipped wood and stone, all generations were wicked in the sight of God, not a man or woman in the whole earth really knew about God. The people of Babel looking for fame with King Nimrod's approval, got together with an idea to build a tower to become unreachable from their enemies and wanted to reign all over the earth from heaven."

In order to stop their behavior and change their direction, God change their language. This change stopped the people of Babel from communicating with each other in building the tower plan for reaching heaven. The disapproval from God notes in Jasper 9:38 " And as the tower which the sons of men built, the earth opened its mouth and swallowed up one third part thereof, and a fire descended from heaven and burned another third, and the other third is left standing," to be a future witness from God's promise seen today.

God's action prevented the people from building the tower and production was destroyed. From the people's actions against God, cause him to scatter the rest of his people with different languages all over the world. Today we can identify with many languages across the world.

Dissilience presented itself even in the time of Noah, where the people had never seen rain, water provided came from the ground during this era, therefore the people had no reason to think otherwise. In this era men and women had little trust in God's ways, but rather trust in themselves, causing wickiness to come between them and God.

The people became more and more wicked, until God's wrath came with anger. The wickiness of their actions caused God to use rain to flood the entire earth and destroy mankind. (Gen: 6:5) "And God saw the wickiness of man was great in the Earth", God also said in (Gen 6:7) "And the lord said "I will destroy man who I have created from the face of the Earth" God created every living thing, destroying life is in God's hand, especially if certain behavioral actions, has threaten his holy methodology.

In the days of the Pharaohs 3000 b.c., had absolute power and represented the Gods of the earth. Pharaohs used their energy to steal treasures from others and bring them back to places like Egypt to gain more power. The Pharaohs greedy thrust for wealth change their culture into a domain of selfishness.

Captivity began a way of life in Egypt and the norms was enslavement. God destroyed those domains when he sent Moses to free the Children of Israel, ending enslavement at that time. Pharaoh's journey to retrieve the Children of Israel cost the Pharaoh's his life, by drowning him in the Red Sea, destroying Pharaoh and liberating his people to freedom.

In America today seems to take us back to the old days of Pharaohs, demonstrating the same attitude only modernizing the culture. The extraordinary experienced the Children of Israel faced was the Red Sea opening up to dry land to escape death. From this horrifying experience you would expect the Children of Israel to be dedicated, loyal, love and trust God forever, but again God's people failed him.

The disobedience of the Children of Israel caused them to wonder in the wilderness for 40 years never reaching the promise God had in store for them, it would have been easier to cooperate with God who had them at their best interest. Image yourself walking around for 40 years with the same clothes and shoes in the wilderness in a foreign land.

In God's Biblical timeline he has always forgiven his people disobedience, Noted in Psalms 85:2 "That has forgiven the iniquity of thy people, thou hast covered all their sins," One day forgiveness will not be given but today forgiveness is still given by God. Noted in ll Chronicles 7:14 If my people which are called by my name, shall humble themselves, and seek my face, and turn from their wicked ways; then will I hear from heaven, and will forgive their sins, and will heal their land.

Remember, the children of Israel did not humble themselves, therefore they wondered in the wilderness for 40 years, a lost generation that died in the wilderness and no chance to the promise land.

BiBLiCaL'S HiSTORY TiMe-LiNe

The world is set-up on God's timeline and only he knows noted in Matthews 24:42 "Watch therefore for ye know not what hour your Lord doth come". End time will erase certain exitance and time will move in God's favor. God created time to find and produce a holy people for his kingdom, where eternal life will come. God's objective is for men and women to make an earthly transformation to a mental spiritual being, meeting expectations and following God's theology on earthy ground.

Biblical mythological messages explains how God gave men and women power to create and provide for self. History has shown us over and over again, when men and women has become impowered by God, they will still find themselves planning a different agenda, creating an agenda away from God expectations. Noted in Jasper 22:49 "And when thou givest them the thing which they require from thee; they set at their ease, and forsake thee and they remember thee no more" time and time again men and women have turned their backs to God and not their face as a symbol of resistant to the truth.

Messages from Adam and Eve experience, should be tattooed in your mind, the human trail previously mentioned started with Adam and Eve who were made in God's image. Adam and Eve being made in his image gave them priority and a measure of glory, which had degrees to advancing and building a closer relationship with God.

This same philosophy of building a relationship with God even stands today for all men and woman to have a personal relationship with God.

The story of Adam and Eve had great impact, a corner stone in Biblical history. The garden of Eden once again,was considered paradise living, a luxuriant place. living in peace, comfort and reaping the fruits of the earth. God commanded both of them not to eat from the fruit on the tree of Knowledge of good and evil, by being disobedient the garden of Eden no longer existed for both. (Genesis 3:23)" Therefore the Lord God sent him from the Garden of Eden, to till the ground" again the people failed God's expectation.

God's journey is still alive and kicking to find a people for his kingdom. During the generation of Adam, God gave man a long-life span. Adam's generation lived to be over 900 years old, American history books identifies Methuselah as the oldest man ever lived in history, the Bible also tells us that Methuselah lived to be 969 years old,a descended of Adam's generation. Due to man's ungodly desires and behaviors becoming too extreme, where men looked towards their own daughters, who they married. An example is located in (Gen: 6:2) "That the sons of God saw the daughters of men that they were fair and they took them wives of all which they choose",

In our society today, we have laws that prevent incest interactions between father and daughter. God highly disapproves of this type of interactions with Adam's generation, which became ungodly acts. God's judgement for Adams generation is noted in (Genesis 6:3) "And the lord, said, my spirit shall not always strive with man, for that be also in flesh, yet his days shall be a hundred and twenty years", God's judgement took away long life spans,like Methuselah and shorten man's life span because of their ungodly acts.

Moving forward on God's timeline, wickiness was extremely rising at a fast pace in the land, until God responded (Gen:6:6)"And it repented the lord, that he made man on earth and it grieved him at his heart" At this point God totally disapproved of the behavior of both men and women which God identifies as wrongful living.

Corruption was thick as thieves and out of control during the time of Noah, God has maximum power to destroy anything and anyone (Gen 6:8) "And the lord said "I will destroy man whom I have created from the face of the earth." God chose Noah for the assignment to destroy the earth, because God trusted Noah, (Genesis 6:9) " These are the generation of Noah was a just and perfect in his generations and Noah walked with God". God trusted Noah to carry out his demands. (Gen 6:13) The people in this era never saw rain before, so Noah warning was ignored by the people and all life was lost.

God started new life after Noah era, with Abraham, choosing him to be the founder of God's new nation, naming him "Father of all nations". God was pleased by Abraham's dedication and worship. Abraham even commanded his children and household to serve the lord in a compassionate, righteous ways and uphold moral justice.

As the new world formed and the greatness of Abraham's generation unfolds to move life forward, God heard of the horrific ungodly acts of men and women in the two cities called Sodom and Gomorrah. God discussed the accusation about the two cities with Abraham. Abraham knew about the power of God and became concerned for the righteous who also live there and spoke out to God (Gensis18:23) "And Abraham drew near, and said "Witt than also destroy the righteous with the wicked? God after having much discussion with Abraham told Abraham if he could find 10 righteous people in the two cities, he would not destroy the two cities and Abraham could not find 10.

Before God destroyed the two cities, Lot and his family was allowed to leave, so Lot gathered his wife and two daughters. God's angel instructed Lot and his family not to look back as they left Sodom and Gomorrah, as the cities were being destroyed. The temptation was too much for Lot's wife for the desires of lust, she turned and looked back and was turned into a pillow of salt. (Gen.19:24) "Then the lord rained upon Sodom and Gomorrah with brimstone and fire from the lord out of heaven "Destroying the inhabitant of the city" Some temptations in life can cost you your life depending on the pay master.

One of God's greatest triumph ever known in Biblical history were God's demand to deliver the Children of Israel out of the hands of the Egyptian Pharaoh. God spoke to Moses from a burning brush and told him to go to Pharaoh and lead the Children of Israel out of Egypt. Image today a burning brush talking to you, if you know anything about your God he talks to some, it simply depends how close your relationship is with God. Always remember he will compensate with you if you establish yourself with him.

This lesson from God was a challenging situation because Pharaoh was a hard pay master and was determine to keep the Children of Israel in slavery. Pharaoh did not know he was actually going against a real God. By Pharaoh determination not to obey, lead to a succession of 10 dreadful plaques sent by God through Moses. The last plague had a divesting impact on Pharaoh, God called for the death of every first born which included Pharaoh's first born. The Israelite spreaded lamb's blood above their door was saved from death. After the death of Pharaoh's first born, he told Moses to take your people and go and they went.

On their route to freedom Moses and the Children of Israel would face two great challenges. Pharaoh's army who were moving rapidly behind them, instructed by Pharaoh to bring them back and the Red Sea which was in front of them. Facing a sea that was 220 miles wide, an impossible task to cross in the eyes of man but not God. With the Children of Israel backs against the wall, Moses instructed by God to stretch out his rod over the Red Sea, at God's command, the Red Sea opened up with the burning wind to dry the surface to reach the other side to safety.

After the crossing of this unbelievable task, the Lord descended to the top of Mount Sinai and call Moses to the top of the mountain. God spoke to the people and reminded them who brought them out of bondage in the land of Egypt.

The Israelites had no patience to know their direction for the new land, when Moses had not returned from the mountain, the betrayal was led by Aaron who also was a part of the crusade with Moses, when he was declaring demands to Pharaoh to let God's people go.

Aaron help the Israelites build the golden calf from the jewels they had with them.

A golden calf was their temporary God only for a moment, but when God found this had occurred, he was very anger, simply because he had sent the laws of the land by Moses for his people to be governed by. Today our timeline will also be a part of making Biblical history through the eyes of Christianity a history only God knows the direction of men or women.

CHRISTIAN METHODOLOGY

america has built a great country, the greatest country in the world, an unbreakable foundation that some have tried to destroy. American forefathers started building with a power greater than themselves and with the love for America defeated and conquer all foreign agents that tried to bring her down.

American people have a definite idea who created the universe, Christianity were formed in representation of Christ like holy living. Christianity began around the first century after Christ died, Christianity has been woven in the fabric of America and other parts of the world. America used this theology called Christianity, an Institution to bring faith and belief to forming and shaping greatness in building a foundation called Democracy.

Christianity is based on a personal teaching of Jesus Christ who came from Nazareth. Christianity focuses on loyalty to trust in Christian beliefs and practices. Christianity is still the most adhered religion in America, Individuals that believe in Christianity creates a sense of quality characteristics and carries the symbolic name of Saints or Christians.

Where you assemble yourself for worship it becomes a personal preference, but it is very important how you surround yourself with the true living word. How does Americans go against their own Christian Institution, an institution with empowerment to make America a great nation and not include God?

You might ask yourself where did Christianity start? Historians tell us that it started after the death of Christ. Christianity came from the ministry of Jesus Christ, it was a new spiritual practice for mankind which became a threat for the status que. Remember during Jesus's walk, people faced the worshiping of Idol Gods, kings, queens and pharaohs, the worshiping of human beings.

How great are we as Americans when we lose focus on who made us a great nation? God is the greatest power that ever existed. Historians tells us that God was the creator of the universe and the start of Christianity. America started participating in the Puritan ethnics, which set up permanent foundations in America's growth.

The Puritan came to America as a non-separationist group who set partnerships with migrates in Massachusetts. Puritans came to America to explore and look for opportunity, making money and spreading the practices of their religion. The Puritan's philosophy was to promote undemented education and improve social and economic life.

Hard work signifies one's salvation and pleasing to God. Their Ideology was teaching the basic reading, writing and arithmetic to create self-reliance and create an economic life style. Puritans stood on promoting good ethnics such as honesty, responsibility, hard work and self-control. The Puritan's concept leads the way on building religious truth in America.

America the beautiful built a melting pot, used as a monocultural metaphor for a heterogeneous of different nationalities of Immigrates, bringing cultures to assimilate in sharing the same sweat, blood and tears all coming together in building this great nation. In American hearts they knew they were apart of building a new growing nation called America.

Frederic Augite Bartholdi also contributed to America by designing the statue of Liberty in 1876 "Liberty Enlightening the World", this statue was given by the French to America to represent being a universal freedom advocate for all people.

The statue of Liberty represented the mother of exile, welcoming millions of Immigrants embodying hope and opportunity for those who seek a better life. The statue came with a friendship between France and America sharing the same philosophy "The state of being free with society from oppressive restriction imposed by authority on one's own life".

Historians tells us it was a promise by the American people to respect and be loyal to the U.S. of America, allegiance to one nation under God, invisible with liberty and justice for the red white and blue flag, filling the sky's with symbolic meanings, representing what America stood for. A pledge of allegiance to the United States of America and its republic for which **all Americans** stand for.

The American flag that fly's all over America, President Eisenhower engaged the congress to add "In God we Trust" showing Americans faith in God. In God we trust is also an official motto of the United States, adapted by Congress in 1956. America even symbolizes their currency with "In God We Trust" Americans during that time loved their country and wasn't afraid to exercise the love for God.

There were other great leaders that made a Godly difference in making America a free world. In the mix were people like Abraham Lincoln, Sojourner Truth, The Roosevelts, The Kennedy's, Shirley Chisholm, Johnson, The Clintons, The Obamas, Martian Luther King, Ghani, Malcolm X, and supreme court justice Ginsberg, their leadership ringed all over the world for justice just to name a few.

Ray Charles strong beautiful lyrics describes great America, singing "America the Beautiful, "But now wait a minute, I am talking about America, you know God done shed grace on thee, he crowned thy good, yes he did, in brotherhood to heal us back again". We must stand in the right lanes together to be healed again, together for humanity among brothers and sisters and keep God in our hearts. Always remember we must walk in a natural and spiritual human being harmonizing as one.

Good Book

The Bible can be your most important tool of reference to achieve a healthier life style. The Bible has been used to set up orders of cultural living, since the time of human exitance. The Good Book is a tribute in the process of the growth of America, using all scriptures to strengthen in designing a healthy lifestyle, noted in ll Timothy 3:16 "All scriptures is given by inspiration of God and is profitable for doctrine, for reproof, for collection for instruction in righteousness."

When you say you believe in the Bible, then you are responsible for its reading and you must cover all of its materials yourself, which takes time. People sometimes say "Rome was not built in a day," therefore bible knowledge takes time to conquer, but it has many, many rewards.

The scriptures of the Bible have its own Institution, referred to as a guide to daily living. The scriptures can Institutionalized your mind to corrective thinking and navigate your progress through scripture reading consistently to better know the course you can take in life.

The Bible is on America's best seller's list every year and has the authority to be used as a prophecy guide in Biblical history and its way to future living. Spiritual living should not be **excluded when answering** questions about natural living but **included** to help guide your natural welfare.

In Biblical writing God chose excellent writers to teach, explain and describe his theology. The Bible has been written over 2,700 years ago, releasing true and factual information that reveals different types of characters, behaviors and actions of human beings.

The Bible speaks of man's consequences for what he or she does during their given life time. Noted in John 14:15 " If you love me, you will keep my commandments" so this is your message " Do it right to get it right" for the Bible covers the entire life span of men and women's past and present daily living.

The strong hold God has on natural living is his demands for righteousness and an end to unrightful living. The Bible offers a solitary of truth to living life experiences, even if you choose to ignored it.

During the pioneer years when America was being tame from the lawless frontier. In the early days the Bible was referred as the **"Good Book** "used to govern the early days of the frontier, even laws were centered around the usage of the 10 Commandments in determining right and wrong. Even today we as a society pattern laws in similar manner as" Thou shall not steal" quoted from the Bible, there are also laws set up against stealing in our society.

Praying in the early days were also essential towards family's workmanship and empowerment to succeed in shaping America. During the early pioneer years God's trust was well respected. People in the pioneer days named their children from the Bible such as John, James, Matthews, Ruth, Easter, Peter and Mary. In the past Bible days, people respected their belief in God, they included God in everyday living because all they had was their strength, blood, sweat and tears and their God to pave their way.

The bible holds its own responsibility to building life, its used like the breath your breve. From the roots of the Bible came doctrines to governed our society today. The world is now wearing a new face empowered by man's gains in wealth, which causes a decrease in daily worship and the Bible hidden away in a cabinet somewhere.

Today "There is no love in the club, membership is closed and the waiting list is forever." You must develop and belong to your own club and understand your journey to fight for freedom here in America, where God has blessed this nation and this is "**home**."

Lateral thinking is also important when exploring the Bible scriptures, because some of the events are 2,700 years old. Lateral thinking helps your imitation visualize things in the subconscious not yet focused on. Lateral thinking also helps give a clear picture of events in the Bible, otherwise cannot be seen at the present but has happen, to obtain spiritual imagination you have to think outside of the box to get a clear picture.

To start this journey, you will not need any money just courage, acceptable reading skills and an open mind to learn. Before you take this journey with God you must have a clear understanding of his theology, his doctrine, his services and how to use these components for the betterment of one's welfare and keeping his promise to his people.

God's doctrine is" One for all and all for one" his teaching and messages should be used to function as one people, we call this movement in America team work or unity. The secret of obtaining the promise from God is your personal relationship, the stronger the relationship the stronger the promise. You have to know God for yourself, this will be a personal relationship between you and God.

Wanting to know God is an investment, it's a choice because you have to be committed, ready for demonstrating accountability and responsibility towards being loyal to your investments and agreements with God.

New pathways must come completely with an open-mind for learning about a power that has always existed. The reading is designed to show you what makes the world go around in America today. In the readings along the way, you will find that men and women will always want to up-root God's theology and replace it with their own confusion, drama and chaos.

God is the only **Super Power** that exist in the universe, a **Spirit** that created heaven and earth. God is looking for a people, documented in the **Good Book's scriptures.** The earth exitance will not be forever and will be replaced with **God's kingdom**.

Looking Deeper

Before you take another step, you have to look deeper within yourself to make your own decision to **believe** in the exitance of God, his theology and doctrines that carries his words. If you continue to seek the knowledge of God always remember, Jesus has made it clear (John 10:30) **"I and my father are one".**

It's hard to believe in God because we are conditioned to only believe in what we see, but if you know God, he moves in things we cannot see. Noted in Hebrews 11:6 "But without faith it is impossible to please him; for he that cometh to God must believe that he is a rewarder of them; that diligently seek him.

God shows himself in three ways "as Father, Son and Holy Spirit. Each has its own functions united as one God. A good example of one being the same is water, which forms in different ways, such as ice and stream, but still considered water, they may have different functions, but at the end of the day it arrives from water.

Something else to consider before you decide to take this walk with God. There are some important factors to examine, who is God? his purpose, powers, doctrine and The **Promise**.

The number one most important factor in reaching your goal for better living is building your own personal portfolio and relationship with God. God makes it clear that each one of us are responsible for carrying his or her own cross. God states in the bible "Take up his cross and follow me." Always remember that you will be accountable for self in the eyes of God and you can't say "Mikey made me do it". It's just not accepted by God or the law of the land (Society).

Exploring the full content of all messages provided, can be a beginning to a clear understanding about the truth to living both naturally and spiritually in one's environment. You must re -educate yourself, remember your society has abandon you for ungodly reasons, therefore Its time to increase self-learning for every American, learning takes place through seeking collective knowledge.

The Gospels

In the New Testament God chose unique authors to write the four gospels in an exploratory overview of Jesus mission on earth. These men who were chosen to write the books of the gospel had interesting back grounds, their characteristics among many stemmed from education, medicine, and finances. You will find the best knowledge and description of Jesus found in the four gospels.

God chose these men for kingdom work, he inspired his four writers and gave them gifts to composed true holy theology. God totally trusted and inspired his chosen writers to record the life of Christ. Jesus 's walk has been noted in the books of Matthews, Mark, Luke and John. God commanded the truth be known to his people in a land of kings, Pharaohs and Idol worshipers.

Synoptic pattern of writing was used among the four writers, where authorships had great similarities incorporated in a common view. Their writing illustrated the artistic birth of Jesus Christ, his sinless passion for life, crucifixion and resurrection. Jesus was made human, a pure reflection of what God wanted men and women to see to accelerate God's mission.

God begins his transformation to build his everlasting kingdom represented by Jesus Christ, who came as an example of the flesh and also made in the image of God. Jesus was an example God gave man and woman to pattern their lives after. Jesus was a perfect example of morally, teaching love, healing and prayer.

Jesus is a witness of God's holiness, Jesus has no doubt in what his purpose is about. Noted in Rev 1:5 " And Jesus Christ who is a faithful witness, and the first of the forgotten of the dead, and the prince of the Kings of the earth. " Now you know, Jesus was chosen to carry God's commissions of change.

During Jesus's travel through the period of the 4 Gospels, Jesus spent time expressing love and passion for his disciples (John 13:23). " Jesus performed many signs and wonders in the present of his disciples to make known that he is the Messiah, the son of God" teaching God's word, giving instructions on how to strive for eternal life, and looking forward to another life with no blemishes or flaws to external living.

God made sure his disciples were ready for the assignment given, noted in John 3:22 "After these came Jesus and his disciples into the land of Judea and there he tarried with them and baptized and preparations were being made to spread the gospel all over the world."

Always remember Jesus also suffered by the hands of man noted in I Peter 2:21 " For even hereunto were ye called; became Christ also suffered for us, leaving us an example". Jesus set up holy men needed to spread his word even after his ratification to his resurrection."

God depended on his disciples to give truthful description of the gospel of Jesus's walk on earth. The four writers also gave the reader an eye witnessed prospective views on current events during the era of Jesus experiences during his time on earth. Basically, the four writers witness some of the same content of spiritual history.

Reading the 4 gospels allows you to help make changes in your life for a clear connection between Jesus and God as one. In the gospels you will find Jesus's experience, a true witness to actual dialog of Jesus speaking. Then said Jesus unto his disciples, "If any man will come after me, let him deny himself, and take up his cross, and follow me." Holy doctrine brings results, noted in Deuteronomy 32:2 " My Doctrine shall drop as the rain, my speech shall distill as the dew, as the small rain upon the tender herb, and as the showers upon the grass. "holy messages ruled the universe under God's watch.

God is the supreme being, creator and the principle of prayer, he is Omnipotent (all powerful) having all power over eternal exitance. Noted in Psalms 47:7 " For God is King of all the earth: sing ye praises with understanding." God is a spirit noted in **John 4:24 God is a spirit** and they that worship him must worship him in spirit and truth".

The last book God provides teaches men and women towards everlasting life, a true review of God's final timeline is revealed in the book of Revelation. Revelation is an apocalypse symbolic vision that reveals a set of history in the form of a final outcome. Revelation is a prophesy of God's living word written through a prophet. The tribulation of Revelation is to choose between being faithful or unfaithful to God's doctrine, time is up for compromises. Revelations is the spiritual realities hidden behind our material world that must come to final judgement.

Truth maybe hard to deal with because we have lived so long with the un-trues of life and its practices, a false replacement mechanism is being used as the truth to conquer or control another under false pretense. The book of Revelations maybe hard to digest but it will come to pass whether you accept the knowledge or not, you won't be able to stop what God has promised.

The last book in the Bible is a prophetic book, explaining the mysteries that had been hidden, revealing who has the supreme power to rule all people. God chooses a man call John for the task of writing his plan to reveal the experiencing of torment and domination of a people whose hearts have harden against the people he loves. God told John to (Rev 1:19) "Write the things thou hast seen and the things which are, and the things which shall be hereafter," Those writings explained the horrific events men and women will experience before the final destination of the world.

John's writing also summarized the different occurrence of deaths for the unrighteous and a presentation of expectations of enteral life for the righteous, who endured and maintained his theology until the end of time.

From the past to the present, God has shown warning indicators to men and women, both in biblical and earthly timelines of his promise of judgments. Your conviction will be handed down like the authority of the Supreme Court in America. The only thing to know, when this time comes, God will have the power not the supreme court.

In the book of Revelation reveals that no one will escape judgement, God also warns the shepherds, gate keepers and the head of God's domains, one who represents God's holiness. The message to the shepherds and the gate keepers mentioned in Revelation, God is warning them, that they are falling short of their messages of wholesome truth about God's living word and the love for his God's people. In due time if the living word is not followed, their candle will be blown out!

The message in Revelation is the most important message in the Bible because at some point, each one of us will have to decide to live for Christ or die as prophecy has spoken. God's coming strictly focuses on life and death for all people and a heavenly beginning for God's chosen people. Revelations simply explains what God does to reach his goal, the search will be finally over in looking to find his **Holy** people for the new Jerusalem to provide beauty and extraordinary external living as he promised.

CHALLENGING POWERS

The world has finally admitted that Satan really is a true negative spirit in the world's orbit and has deeply seeded himself in the human minds, initiating negative thinking and behavior that leaves negative consequences.

The damages negative powers have created has left the world with a clear path of what we don't want participating in our lives. Satan has shown himself in the minds of our government officials in the last several years, controlling figures governing the American money for themselves and stealing the integrity of the working class and the people they serve.

The actions of these negative forces feeding negative behaviors is trying to ruin your life and set up road blocks against your success., These negative actions have become a sour eye for the American people. It is very important to become aware of the two strongest powers in the world that has control over lives, a positive power and negative power which can live in our souls and direct our paths.

The source of power lies in two hands, God and Satan, both rule the day and night. Man's power only lies in his or her choices that feeds off good or evil. This message is not a comparison between two powers God's or Satan's. A clear understanding from Biblical historians has produced the evidence, who created the world, **"God"** who has power over all natural or spiritual exitance let's be clear on that. God created Satan or the Devil for man or woman to have a choice of the type of life worth living.

When we explained to society about Satan's forces in a spiritual way that effects daily living, even President Biden of 2021 also identified demonic spirits with the Trump world and mention America must act to rid the demonic spirits surrounding the White House and move forward gaining back love in kindness to the United States of America.

Some People somehow ignore or refuse to identify the exitance of Satan power that affect our everyday life. Americans depend on science to identify existences and provide the solution to any of our occurrences in life and if science can't prove its exitance, then it does not exist for the human man.

Satan's theology has woven its self in our society through different entities, such as the big screen movies Industries. Classic demonic Movies has earned over $108 million at US box offices and $193 million worldwide producing horror, satanic and scary movies.

Movies like Rosemary's baby designed to spook you and give you a terrorizing message of demonic spirits. Primeval, a warlord named Lucifer and his demonic activities, Candyman who demonstrated that he had supernatural spirits terrorizing his victims. Chuckie the demonic child whose behavior demonstrates the killing of others.

The biggest movie remembered, that made notice of demons was the Exorcist (1973) making over 232.9 million at the box office, this movie reflected on demons inducing and possessing infestation of demonic behaviors. In 2017 horror films like the Movie "It" grossed $700,381.75 at the box office, horror movies coming at you before you can blink an eye and is flooding the markets.

In America we celebrate a tradition every year called Halloween, the tradition started in ancient Celtic festival of Samhain pagan culture, who believed that spirits from the dead was able to come back to harm people in the physical world, they put on customs to ward of ghost and spirits.

We have to be careful on the comment of Halloween because the stakeholders are our children. America spends over $10.14 billion dollars a year to make this tradition happen. The season host gobblers, bats, ghost, skeletons, witches, devils and haunted houses all enjoyed by our American societies.

Let's stay on the safe side of Halloween because our children are the beneficiaries of this celebration and the reward of the holiday, that brings sharing of candies and parties, only children think about. You must know the facts on what we worship in our societies to understand the consequences of actions people copycat, can be influenced by the activities you engage in.

We embrace the idea of demonic spirits by what we are exposed to and conditioned to think. Whether it holds truth or not, we have to be careful how information is reflected towards negative forces, only because people who suffer with negative mental illness, their actions and behaviors are now on the rise as a negative force in our societies identified as mental disabilities, too afraid to think of demonic behavior. How do a person become a murder suspect holding professional degrees in criminology and kill 4 Idaho students to exercise curiosity against human beings?

The mental diagnose for violence is becoming normal, when an 18-year-old is found gunning down 19 children and 2 adults in a Texas school setting. In Buffalo New York 10 people killed by another 18-year-old at a super market. Hate crimes entering the soul at rapid speed and Satan is for filling his goal to destroy the minds of the people, by behaving in a forceful way which destroys lives on the way. Satan becomes your opponent, who has no love for God, but a strong desire of revenge on God's people. Satan is a virus spreading negative spirits all around the universe with no cure insight.

Guns in the hands of children killing children, The fifteen-year-old boy charge will multiple counts of murder on four students in the Michigan Oxford school shooting. Inquiring minds want to know, where are these kids getting these guns? Are guns being sold and distributed under the corner of your local gas stations? Demonic spirits are entering the minds of our children because of extreme negative exposure, that children have not yet matured for guns.

Our society have suffered enough with people like Manson'

Cults who created ritualistic killing, where minds were condition to kill over and over again. Jonestown massacred people, who got caught up with bad conditions and was looking for a Savior, but instead were poisoned and life was lose.

Ted Bundy who went on a massive killing and cannibalism spree, The Boston strangler who preyed on killing women, and the brutal killing of 4 students at Idaho University, just to name a few. The negative force that surrounds us today is a reality, Satan is real my friend whether you accept it or not.

In France in Oct 29, 2020 an Islamic terrorist beheaded a woman and killed two other crying out to his God in honor of his terrorism "Allah Abu (God is greatest) would God call for the beheading of human beings? demonic minds have powers too.

Lucifer has a true Biblical history and names as Satan or Devil, a spirit that once dwelled in heaven, Lucifer was created by God noted in Ezekiel 28:15 "Thou were perfect in thy ways from the day thou were created, till iniquity was found in thee" Lucifer had great beauty as a man angel, he was one of God's most beautiful angel God had ever designed. Lucifer became impressed by his own beauty, intelligence, power and position, began to glorify himself rather than give his creator the glory.

Lucifer had an ultimate revenge against God being threw out of heaven, humiliated and strip of his heavenly powers. Lucifer who transformed into Satan characteristics maintained certain powers, after being thrown out of heaven, noted in Isiah 14:12 "How art thou fallen from heaven Lucifer, son of the morning star! how are cut down to the ground, which did weaken the nation "to cause disruptions in everyone's life."

Always remember Satan has no power when it comes to God, Satan with his bold feelings and extraordinary speech is second to God, stated in Isaiah 14:13 " I will ascend into heaven, I will exalt my throne above the stars of God: I will sit also upon the mount of the congregation, in the sides of the North and the Devil continues in Isaiah 14:14 " I will ascend above the heights of the clouds; I will be like the highest." Satan wanted God's position but he was not powerful enough to take it from God, so Satan works to destroy his people.

The devil knows God loves his people to maintain divine spiritual order. The Devil roams around God's people carrying a disease, a spreader of deception, causing distraction, disruption and to redirect people to self-destruct, this pleases Satan to stop the building of God's Kingdom in Individuals' hearts.

Satan has a supernatural spirit you normally can't see, but Satan will allow some to see him working. Satan loves to reflect negative experiences in your mind on a continuous base to remind you of your regrets and the dark side of life experiences.

Satan deeply seeded mechanism can penetrate your thought process, blocking the mind with continuous negative thoughts about yourself and your unfavorable experiences involving sorrows, regrets, hatred, revenge, dislikes and abandonment.

If your dark side of life becomes extreme, then medical science recognizes the dark side of life's negative aggression, as a justification of a case of mental illness and those dark experiences can become the act of schizophrenia.

The truth of the matter, visual images of Satan can appear in certain individuals subconscious. Satan is identified as a negative supernatural power and when the pressure gets too heavy you will hear someone say, the old saying "The Devil made me do it"

You must understand the power of this negative supernatural spirit because it plays an important part in your life. The brain is the most highly functional piece you own in your body, it is your command center, heart of your cognitive thinking process and all thoughts take place in the brain.

Satan is like a snake when devouring his prey, he will swallow the head of his victim first, therefore Satan also swallows the human brain. Satan knows as long as he can control your thought patterns, he will stay in control of your destiny. Satan knows he does not have total power to control you, by having his own experience against God.

Satan fought against God with his negative behavior and his

limited power, caused Lucifer to be thrown out of heaven with his crew of angles who also defied God. Satan is not looking for his own Kingdom, his mission is to take over to destroy the power of God's Kingdom.

Satan's specialty is to develop negative traits in human being without their permission, a force using negative character traits of jealousy, envy, hatred, arrogant, selfishness, high-mindedness and bad attitudes just to name a few. When these types of characteristic enter the heart, you become stone cold and love is locked out, love has little to no chance of getting in.

Satan can retrieve the body to feel weak, worthless, helpless and doomed. This type of feeling blindsides the truth about who you really can be. Remember once Satan filtrates in your mind, he becomes comfortable knowing he has control, he will leave demons to monitor you, as he moves to his next victim using the same plan to steal, kill and destroy an execution of one's life.

Satan wants his power to have a negative effect on your worship with God because he is running out of time. We are closely approaching the revealing of God 's real purpose for his people. One day this madness will be all over according to God.

Man is accelerating the unrevealing of the last book called Revelation. . . God's authority speaks in Rev 16:17 "And the seventh angel poured out his vial into the air and there came a great voice of the temple of heaven, from the throne saying it is done! The message is clear, when God says its enough man's power will completely disappear and God's power will be activated forever.

How can we not recognize the existence of God, when America and across the world celebrates the tradition of Easter every year, Easter is a part of our historical history. Easter celebration acknowledges the purpose of Jesus Christ. The great comforter, using his power to healed the sick and raised the dead. Jesus the forgotten son rose from the dead for everyone to see the power of God.

The attitudes of men and women today, lack consistency to participate in today's spirituality for effective living? You think the power of God's word stops today? Especially during the period of

Jesus's walk on earth, looked upon as a memory and celebration only, then back to business as usual with no participation until next Easter.

The world must wake up and smell the cappuccino on these messages, remember the history of Jesus Christ should have a permanent affect in your life, if it doesn't you have let man deceive you. noted in Matthew 24 4-5 And Jesus answered and said unto them, take heed that no man deceives you, (5)" For many shall come in my name, saying, I am Christ and shall deceive you"

Jezebel negative powers

God show all sides of evil doers, individuals that work against his Holiness, he also shows examples of women working with demonic spirits against humanity. This example is just to remind us that ugliness can also lie in women. A woman has a powerful tool called persuasion, she can use her mental or physical persuasion to change a person's decisions from right to wrong.

In Bible history a woman with persuading credentials, her name was **Jezebel**, she was a phenomenal princess in the 9th century, she was an evil queen married to King Ahab of Israel. Whatever she desired she received, even if it involved murder. Jezebel had Naboth stoned to death to take ownership of his vineyard. Jezebel also had a hand in the murdering of the Yahve prophets, (1 kings 18:13) "Was it not told my lord what I did when jezebel slew the Prophets of the lord" Jezebel powers extended in allowing individuals to practice ritual sex, fornication and temple prostitution. she was a hum dinger during her time.

Jezebel's God was nature which is considered Pagan Gods, she hated the Monotheistic Hebrew religion and her efforts were to change the kingdom of Israel from a Hebrew environment to a Pagan environment. Jezebel had great influence over King Ahab causing him to protect Pagan worshiper, a violation of God's Holiness which cause God to bring a three-year drought on the land because of non-humanitarian behaviors.

Jezebel's characteristics has become symbolic in human behavior, God warned the church of Thyatira, Jezebel type behavior using false prophetess and misleading in fornication (Rev 2:20)" Notwithstanding I have a few things against thee, because thou suffer that woman Jezebel, which calleth herself a prophetess, to teach and to seduce my servants to commit fornication, and to eat things sacrificed unto Idols"

Jezebel's wickiness had no repentance, noted in (I kings 2:21-23)" And I gave her space to repent of her fornication: and she repent not (22-) "Behold I will cast her into a bed, and them that commit adultery with her into great tribulations, except they repent of their deeds. Verse 23 says "And I will kill her children with death: and all the churches shall know that I am he which searches the rein and heart; and I will give unto every one of you according to your works" this is the real truth about the woman Jezebel.

Often today when people see women demonstrating negative behavior in a seductive way, they refer her behavior as Jezebel, also back in the day they call seductive women, salon girls, street walkers or prostitutes the daughter of Jezebel, all who had unfavorable behavior (all kings 9:10)" And the dogs shall eat, in the portion of Jezebel, and there shall be done to bury her." God is not playing when it comes to his promises and his actions, he seeking a kingdom for the last time during the last days, until than we must still support the ways of righteous humanity until God says time is here.

PROPHETIC SIGNS

God's play book is available for everyone to read, called the Bible. God uses his play book to governor his people on earth's holy ground. In God's play book there is a prophetic blueprint guide to earthly living. God's theology reveals his holy doctrine with instructions that explains his principles and guidelines to humanity and worship. (numbers 14:8)" If the Lord delight in us, then he will bring us into this land, and give us a land which flowered with milk and honey" meaning he will provide you with the best of life here on earth.

Self-managing is a major part of having choices, you must take steps in the right direction on how your life should be as a human being. I would not exclude God out of the equation in developing your lifestyle, remember, God created the world not man. God's intention some day is to dwell permanently with his holy people in a holy eternal place. Your faith and worship blossom's your spirituality in being a part of that holy place.

God gives men and women a free will to participate in his theology, but you must do the right thing and know the definition of right and wrong, remembering all choices and decisions has consequences good or bad.

He is the Alpha and the Omega meaning " The beginning and the end". It is written in the Bible that God is a jealous God and put no other God before him, this is a fact written in stone. (Nahum

1:2) "The lord is a jealous and avenging God the lord is avenging and wrathful, the lord takes vengeance on his adversaries and keep wrath for his enemies" God will respond to human disobedient and apply judgement".

When we speak about God's wrath or judgement, you need a clear understanding what this means. This is a tool God uses to warn men and women what he holds one responsible for when he sees unfavorable actions in his eyes. God's warnings may be gentle, harsh or even death, depending on what he wants to see happen, remember he has power of life and death. (Roman 1:18) For the wrath of God is revealed from heaven against all ungodliness and unrighteousness of men, who by their unrighteousness suppress the truth"

God has used warning signs and shown supernatural movements all through world's history and its exitance. God created a time line so we can review the past to know what to expect for the future and future generations. God alerts you when his theology is being violated. Faith is King says "If you want the truth, the whole truth, Nothing but the truth so help you God" and can take the bitter with the sweet, then you must understand the full nature of God and how he performs.

Always remember who has the greatest power over the world, God did not create human life for his people to experience oppression, neglect, abuse or discrimination against anyone on this universe.

A wrath can be considered as warning from God that should fuel a person's direction to proper living and worship. Warning and wraths are God's toolbox to confront the objection to holiness. (Jeremiah 30:23) "Behold the storm of the Lord! wrath has gone forth, a whirling tempest: it will burst upon the head of the wicked." The question to answer who is the wicked?

God's natural revelations coincides with spiritual revelations provided for us to see and hear. Revelations for earthly learning is the revealing of something that was hidden and surfaces into exitance. When God feels his principles, authority and positions has been violated he responds by actions. Today's men and women has become egotistical, selfish and unrighteous, which draws God attention to react.

God has provided us with clear evidence, knowledge and examples to alarm or warn us when we lose focus on the real reasons he created life. Signs will consist of super natural occurrences or things we have never known or seen but now becomes reality in one's time of living.

Warning signs have been written in scripture form, noted in Isaiah 28:2 "Behold, the lord hath a mighty and strong one, which as a tempest of hail and a destroying storm, as a flood of mighty waters overflowing, shall cast down to earth with the hand."

In the 21st century most people should know who God is and his purpose (Theology) simple because societies celebrate different events to support the recognition of Jesus Christ and his theology, like Christmas and Easter. Evidence provided by the Bible reveals concrete practices of special occasions sets up guidelines to faith.

Pay attention to natural occurrences we experience today, God allows these unfavorable occurrences that man creates, it's a message, you "reap what you sow." Man's overflow of destruction creates signs of global warning, where gases are trapped between outer atmosphere and earth's atmosphere waiting to poison our air we breathe. Earth surfaces heating up, ice glaciers 2000 ft below the surface of the ice are melting and beginning to overflow the oceans, seas, rivers and lakes causing water to ruin man's constructions.

God's strengths have been shown in rain and winds, Hurricane Doran (2019) a catastrophic destroyer that affected many lives in states as Texas, taking lives than leaving Texas, going to the Bahamas at 150 miles an hour to triumph over Meliora Florida, still unleashing its power in Palm Beach, Melbourne Orlando, Jacksonville, Savannah, Charleston, Wilmington and Raleigh. Immediately behind hurricane Doran came 12 tornadoes touched down including in North Carolina collecting life and land.

Man has no power, but to let hurricanes run its course, there is no stopping a natural revelation, the signs have to be shown to man as a result of his behavior. (2 Peter 2:9) "Then the lord knows how to rescue the Godly from its trials, and to keep the unrighteous under punishment until the day of judgement". Natural occurrence has meaning in the eyes of God, he made the wind and rain to stir up whenever he pleases and the more man disrupts God's order the more signs we see.

When the ground opens up and the environment is destroyed, a good chance it can be an act of God because in the last days when time is whining up he reveals to man in (Rev 16:18) "And there were voices and thunders and lighting, and there was a great rumbling,peals of thunder, and a great earthquake such as was not since men were upon the earth, so mighty an earthquake, and so great." These occurrences will come, as the Coronavirus came in our lives that we never expected to experience.

Individuals also in control of our society need to recognize the signs God makes available, change must happen for the welfare of the people. The people will suffer the consequences from authority's decisions. A great example is Gov. Greg Abbot of Texas following the pathways and kissing the ring of Donald Trump has put Texas in arms way.

The state of Texas paid their consequences through state governor's poor and reckless handling of state matters during the crisis of the Pandemic, where Gov. Greg Abbot did not capitalize on shutting the necessary Industries down and masking up, to stop the spread of Covid 19. The one force the governor was powerless over was the Pandemic, then the Pandemic hit Texas hard. Calamities continues for the Texians, with the killer 20 inches snow and 18 below storm that hit Texas on February 16, 2021.

People all over Texas suffering from freezing weather conditions, complete power shut downs in some areas, outraged water levels, no drinking water because water available had been contaminated with carbon dioxide. Sitting on top of a deadly Pandemic, freezing weather an vaccine outlets shut down all over Texas.

This calamity Texians were experiencing, didn't seem to bother Sen Ted Cruz another Republican Red to opt himself out of the deadly situation by vacating in Can Cancun Mexico. Now isn't he the man of the hour, an authority figure's behavior during America's crisis should be dealt with in only one way, the "Vote" when it's time the evidence is there to say "No" it's all over Casanova.

Gov. Greg Abbott still can't cut the mustard in 2022, sending 12 million dollars of tax payer's hard-earned revenue to bus Migrants to Philadelphia to share the burden of these homeless people because the man in charge has no problem-solving skills to offer Texians for resolution. Gov. Greg Abbott has brought dark nights to the people he is in charge of.

COVID

The big warning signs for Americans and the rest of the world in the 21 century's timeline have committed the same similar acts God warned in past Biblical history. God has judged and destroyed his people in the past, who has fought against the purpose and doctrine of Jesus Christ since the beginning of time. The world is moving more towards the end of God's objectives of his promise, than the people who started with God in the beginning like Adam and Eve and the Children of Israel, who had more time to get it right.

Today America and the world have experienced a monster killing bodily intrusion, a universal crisis holding Americans hostage both mentally and physically, a sense of horror effecting everyday life upon American shores. An erupted volcano, America could not quiet down and hope seemed nowhere around.

The Covid 19 Pandemic of 2020, traveling as an invisible man at rapid speed, choosing to eliminate who he chooses, meanwhile our commander and chief Donald Trump and his Republican Reds has jumped ship to control the virus, instead turned their mission into dividing the country's Democracy.

Man has found himself fighting an invisible power greater than its science a stranger who has snuck into our lives through a transmission, attacking the body, a ghost terrorizing our immune system, weakening our hearts and taking our breath away. This stranger kills with attitude, using social distancing to keep us from each other. Taking charge of our lives and determining life or death. No respect for science who cannot stops it spread, known as Covid 19.

Where it came from, no human really knows only trails of speculations. The Covid 19 shut America down almost to a standstill, as time progressed science knew very little about this Coronavirus, but they did know that wearing a mask, social distancing and washing hands could slow the virus down, but it could not stop the virus from killing.

President Trump was heartless by trying to hide the virus from the American people, lying and being deceitful in the eye of God for the scriptures says "No one who practice deceit shall dwell in my house; no one who utters lies shall continue before my eyes" remember lying lips is abomination to the Lord." Trumps lies put this country on death row, supporting wealth instead of the welfare of the American people as the death angel spreads its wings.

Lying is a betrayal, it violates trust, lies can be damaging and harmful between one another. Ruining trust is beyond repair, its stressful and emotional draining when you become involved with a liar. Truth frees you from dishonesty.

Trumps disposition of lies, continued to set-up road blocks to stop scientists like Dr Fauci and other medical scientists from trying to provide factual medical data to guide the country through the wide spread of the Pandemic. President Trump steadily ignoring the law of science that God provided these professional men and women with the ability to heal the land.

Trump totally refused to lock down the country to help stop the spread of Covid 19. Trump also planted seeds to disrupt the CDC order by staying inside to help stop the spread. Trump also supported businesses to open early when the Pandemic was at its worst. Trump working against maintaining the order of the CDC to a least mask wearing, social distancing and washing hands. Trumps limited knowledge to navigate the virus was present, Trump a nice house but nobody home.

America could have controlled the virus, but the controlled minded republicans continued to play with other people's lives at the cost of following in Trump's parade. A similar act of Jim Jones followers who Kool-aided themselves into death believing in a false Demigod. Inquiring minds what to know during Trumps era was America empowered by Demigod theology, half mortal and half earthly God in mind set only!

This rejection of the Trump parade to stop the spread caused America to suffer in great consequences of death among the American people. This brings a message from the living word noted in Psalms 119:53 "Horror hath taken hold upon me because of the wicked that forsake the Law" God gave us science and our nation's leader ignored the antidote to help stop the spread of the Pandemic early stages. Scientists working diligently trying to figure a strategy to fight the enemy on their own soil and cure the nation.

The real disappointment were the American's people's attitudes during the spread of the Pandemic. A patient less society dealing with an invisible enemy that none could see, but it didn't matter to the people they were spoiled with fruitless activities and could not do without their pleasures and comforts, such as haircuts, nail cosmetics, Indoor recreations, lavish restaurants, bars and physical fitness gyms, nothing essential to surviving to support daily living through the Pandemic. Selfish individuals all over America were putting their loves ones at risk, especially the front-line responders' lives, who maintained medical obligation to receive anyone sick including the selfish Gurus.

If the Coronavirus had a physical army invading American communities by weapons, then I am sure people would not have had a problem staying undercover. A lot of people are so condition by American smoke screens they can't even governor and make decisions for their own healthy living and know when there is a threat on their lives. Don't let Capitol Hill lead you down death row because society wants to play politics with your lives. Ignoring the Pandemic could be a death sentence for you and your family. The only one who really knows the outcome is God, because he can see everything at one time, that's why we call him "God"

The powers of the republican party were too busy trying to

change Democracy into a framework of American dictatorship, rather than to heal its nation. God allowed another calamity to be born, another rebirth of unjustified killing of a African American man, George Floyd, in Minneapolis, Minnesota, a crime of hate had been committed by a white police officer who physically killed him, by applying pressure with his knee for a least 9 mins on Mr. Floyd's neck, cutting his oxygen and blood flow to his brain, while he called for his mother's help who had already passed before his life.

This situation open Panadura's box and caused a worldwide protest, voices ringing across the world for the injustice of all people, but especially for African Americans experiencing the dark side of racism since Africans hit the shores of Virginia as slaves and the property of white Americans. The strong hold on racism seems unbreakable, different forms of slavery has existed since African Americans came to America. Whites will continue to fight to the death to keep control of wealth and others. The American Flag flies over African American heads while they experience death in the street of their communities and the outcome of their death will be ruled justified homicide in the mist of the unrighteous police officers.

The Covid 19 opened up the other side of Panadura's box revealing the unsavory treatment and conditions white Americans had successfully done while riding on the backs of others for generations, to gain their wealth and denied others of healthy living and economic opportunity.

There are white Americans, who has embedded racism in the American fabric and their hearts and refuse to share the American dream with black and brown people. During the Pandemic the rich and its industries made of over 2 trillion dollars in profit. The rich got richer and the poor got sicker, facing death came knocking at the door and the pandemic became our neighbors.

Let's be clear God did not cause the Pandemic, but he allowed it to happen by men and women's own destructive behavior and the maltreatment of his people, caused many to be tested by God. The message here is to repute negative behaviors, trust and use God as your resting place in patience where life gets better. Pay attention to this message given in 2020 Christmas season services by Bishop Lambert Gates Jr says " In teaching we must trust and obey the will of God." The signs from the Pandemic points to trails of Revelations and trust will be needed to overcome the fear.

God provided men and women with earthly ground, to create healthy living during their timeline, but man has continued to destroy the earth until America and the world is facing calamities like climate change, that is ruining the environment surrounding our communities and weakening the stability of the universe. What is clear today, man is destroying what God has made available for healthy living on this earth.

The natural occurrences mentioned are the reasons God will eliminate the wrong of men for the last time, he will not be seeking a people or moving to find another people. God will know his people by their loyalty, God has the final decision to decide who will enter the kingdom. The final outcome will be centered around destroying his adversaries and taken his throne to rule all people he has chosen for ever more.

LONDON BRIDGES PRESIDENT DOWN

When God allows you to govern his people your responsibility becomes accountable for your deeds and actions, noted in Proverbs 16:12 "It is an abomination to Kings to commit wickiness for the throne is established by righteousness.

During the four years of Donald Trump Presidency, he and the Republican Reds were like beast administrating over the nation. Americans went through a period of unpresidential acts of corrupted behavior, allowing Pandora's box once again to open during the Trump era and the terror began to spill out.

President Trump and the Republican Reds tried implementing an autocracy system, a government system designed to reflect possession of unlimited power from one person to governor it's nation. The same type of autocracy government used to rule in Russia, China and North Korea.

The Mueller Report was a complete flop, allowing Attorney General Bill Barr to interpret the finding in Trumps favor, a cop out by Robert Mueller. President Trump being impeached by the House of Representatives lost it way. An impeachment stopped by the republican party, who controlled the senate, violated acts of breaking constitutional policies to allow President Trump to stay in office. The Republican party scratched President Trump's itch in support to uphold Ukraine funding, to pressure Ukraine to get dirt on Vice President Joe Biden to give him an edge to be re-elected in 2020.

The fumes of the Pandemic coming from Pandora's box was not strong enough for President Trump to focus on a deadly Pandemic, America will be facing. The scary thing about this situation, Trump was the first to be notified of the Pandemic's arrival and did nothing to protect the American people.

The "reckoning" for Donald Trump came because of his own reckless behavior turning into negative consequences. President Trump hide the horrific disease that attack and invaded the American people. When Covid 19 Pandemic hit the shores of America, President Trump and the Republican Reds experienced a great derailment, when trying to change America to an autocracy government with republican control.

President Trump leading America down death row by ignoring the Pandemic, sentencing Americans to execution. Trump making murderous decisions causing the American people to become defenseless against a rising killer Covid 19, causing death and fear to rise among the American people. God handles the misconduct of men and women who have great authority. Noted in Proverbs 19:19 " A man of great wrath shall suffer punishment; for if thou deliver him; yet thou must do it again."

God knows if he gives a person like Trump mercy, he would only do it again, therefore God said "Vengeance is mine; said the Lord "noted in Deuteronomy 32:35 " To me belonged vengeance and commence; their foot shall slide in due time; for the day of their calamity is at hand, and the things that shall come upon them"

The Coronavirus was kinder to Trump than he was to his nation, survived the Covid 19 and escaped 2 impeachments, Donald Trump has lost his compass and has become a directionless man. Trump has become toxic and will not surrender the truth, but demonstrates his loyalty to his own survival, no longer bound by the truth but living a lie.

Trump's behavior makes people wonder if he suffers from some kind of mental disorder? Journalist in the free world media, consistently asking does Trump have a narcissistic personality disorder? A dysfunctional mental condition in which people have an inflated sense of focus only on their own importance, a great need for excessive attention, troubled with developing relationships and has no empathy for others. Inquiring minds want to know, are these types of behaviors described scene in President Donald Trump character?

Satan's next assignment is bold and works through Trump and the Republican Reds, who gives the stamp of approval to The QAnon group. Trump saying in his own words " These are people who love our country" A pedophilia (Attracted to children having sexual desires) a disinformation network spreading conspiracy theories to create diversion among Americans people and spread worshipping satanic belief and human child sacrifice, pedophilia behaviors does not love our country, America.

Trump and the Republican Reds continue to allow republican Margorie Taylor Green, **Queen Bee Junkie,** supports QAnon conspiracy theories. The QAnon now have permission to filtrate throughout the republican party and control their direction in Democracy. The republicans supported Margorie. Taylor Green's bold verbal abuse and actions. Margorie Taylor Green works against the true reality of America's experiences, stating a plane from the 911 incident never hit the Pentagon, Clintons were responsible for Jfk Jr. airplane crash, Jews used lasers starting forest fires to make money and the eye opener of the day was her crazy accusation, verbally harassing a high school shooting survivor stating "the shooting never happen." as she walks behind the survivor verbally harassing him.

The actions of republican Marjorie Taylor Greene caused her to be stripped of her seat on the education and budget committee, by the House of Representative by a majority vote. The Republican party's decline to discipline her participation in false conspiracy and unethical behavior, but Instead supported her to stay on the committees. What flows out of one side of her mouth is a humble Christian and the other side she is fighting with the devil by saying "This is Trump's party no one else", leaving no room for other choices.

Trump continue to embrace QAnon's, a home-grown elite network terrorizing group. President Trump still attempts to fuel the efforts of the QAnons to hijack America's conversation. As some would say "Captain Caius is at it again."

Right in front of your eyes demonic spirits have woven itself in the republican party as disciples for former President Trump in the United State Congress. Senator Kevin McCarthy who kisses the ring of Donald Trump has to now make deals with the devil to gain his position as speaker of the house, is digging a grave for some to bury him in while entertaining the very things that poisons our society.

The breakup of the Republican Reds is on God's agenda with more to come you "reap what your sow" Trump stuck on using mind controlling behaviors for his republican supporters. Trump supporters drunk on propaganda, high on aggressive behavior, caught under the spell of false conspiracy theories and causing followers to be caught up on actions of precision to take up radical position against a standing Democracy. Many Republican candidates lost their race in the 2022 midterm election because of their position of being election deniers a well lesson learned. This election was all about the stand for Democracy and American votes for freedom to live in a free world!

The faith to change must be in the eyes of Americans to endure the dark cloud President Trump has caused America to face. A demonizing force, President Trump and the Republican Reds twisted and turned the constitution and bill of rights in every way to create change.

Bernstein gives his views about Donald Trump saying "He is a constitutional criminal (Carl Bernstein political analyst- landscape of Trumpism), Bernstein speaks with authority "Out of control madman", determined to control the mental mind of his followers. Referring to Trump's vicious personality, an enemy to the interest of the United States of America.

The Republican Reds attempted to change America's Democracy, but Americans used their unbreakable faith, stood the test of time and let their vote speak to recovery, London bridges falling down on Donald J. Trump.

When your sins overwhelm your actions and you start to cry out for help or mercy and your violations are against the welfare of God's people, there is no mercy from God. God will certainly turn away from you as the Lord says in Proverbs 1:28 Then shall they call upon me, but I will not answer; they shall seek me early, but they shall not find me".

When demonic spirits are allowed in your life, they have no allegiance to anyone and will cause confusion under the same roof. When you buy into Satan's mischief, you seek self-destruction and it's on its way. Trust in these words the "Devil will always leave you hanging."

"Psalms 140:7 " O God the Lord, the strength of my salvation, thou have covered by head in the day of Battle" Life has certainly been a battle under the Trump administration. A war against the Coronavirus, Democracy and a battle to maintain America freedom.

Trumps objective in his last days in the White house, tried to make America suffer for his loss of the 2020 presidential election. Trump's sole energy were to create division and demonstrate revenge in his loss of his election. President Trump acted against the American people by allowing continuous suffering during the Christmas holidays. Revenge was already set up from his loss of the presidential 2020 election.

Trump warned the people in one of his rallies, "if you choose Biden you won't have a Merry Christmas." During the 2020 Christmas holiday season, Trump showed no interest and turned his back on the American people, needing economic relief during the holiday season, but Trump rather play golf during his holiday season, while Americans struggled with no defense in the necessary living accommodations for survival, such as food, rent protection, unemployment, job lost, domestic despair and virus intrusion.

Demons has filtrated in the minds of some republicans' leaders and supporters fueled by the demonic spirit of President Trump. Trump and the republican party, supports violent attitudes that results in physical and verbal behaviors demonstrated in public places. This behavior is a result of the president's attitude spilling down to his followers. A prime example of violent repercussion of Trump's rhetoric were made active in 2022, when speaker of the house Nancy Pelosi's husband, being attacked at his home by a Trump supporter with a hammer, violent Trumpism still "hanging from the rafters."

Demons are fighting for exitance and leading Americans down a false path, while republicans clinging on to power trying to create division among the American people, an old-time method of divide and conquer orchestrated by Republicans such as Mitch McConnell, Kevin McCarthy and other Republicans Reds.

The Republican Reds still experiencing demonic spirits, floating around, the republican's camp. A good example would be attorney Sidney Powell, chanting to lock up republican Governor Brian Kemp for keeping the oath to the American People. Kemp who acknowledged the legal vote certification to elect Joe Biden the next President of the United States of America.

Trump's campaign lawyer Joe DiGenova verbalizing aggressive behavior, about another Republican Christopher Krebs a cyber security official, saying " He is a Class A moron, he should be drawn and quartered, taken out and shot" this type of rhetoric can turn physically violent. Republicans creating an aggressive culture helping President Trump and his conspiracy theories to undermine America's Democracy.

When Demons filtrates the mind, they have no allegiance to anyone but to try to conquer what they are after. When Satan's work is achieved he leaves behind much chaos causing disorder and confusion. Always remember you are Satan's reward and once he conquers you, Satan is off to find his next assignment.

Division now standing in the right lane, General Attorney Bill Barr and homeland security official, confirms there were no election fraud and only 27 republicans started to face reality and temporary turned to America's Democracy and the rest of the republicans took to the hills to lick their wounds of the loss of their demagogue in the 2020 election.

The sore losing republicans are still hanging around Pandora's box, knocking at the door supporting the lamb duck, psychotic acts of Donald Trumps to overturn the decision of losing the presidential election and to spread the lie that Donald Trump did not lose his election.

Steadily spreading fake news were Georgian Republicans Lin Woods and Sidney Power extend themselves at a rally for the

Georgian run-off election to be held in January 2021. The two republicans expressed to the people that the elections will be rigged and not to vote. These types of conversations seem to commit to division, that successfully made John Owosso Jewish American, Son of a Jewish immigrate and Rev Warnock Pastor of Evaenisa Baptist Church a following Pastor of Martin Luther King Jr, both winners of the 2021 run off in Georgia.

One of the last dervish maneuvers of President Trump murderous decisions fueled an Insurrection on Capitol hill. Congressmen and women on both parties were in a session of presidential certification in an attempt to change powers of presidency. In the eyes of Donald Trump there were no acceptance of a loss of the 2020 presidential election, even a former republican Governor Chris Christe mentions that "Donald Trump is all about me" who also got off the little red school bus, riding into a fueling Insurrection!

Proverbs notes that "The Tongue has the power of life and death" Trumps exercised this biblical expression, at his rally nearby the White House, he verbally said " We will walk down Pennsylvania ave" talking to domestic terrorist groups to encourage them to siege the Capitol and overthrow America's presidential election.

This act undercuts the nation's Democracy, an attempt to stop the certification of the new elected President Joe Biden. Spiritual similarities identify Trumps attitude in Proverb 28:10 "Whoso causes the righteous to go astray in an evil way; he shall fall himself into his own pit." a self-designed pit for the notorious Donald J. Trump.

The rally on January 6,2021 were fueled also with Giuliani shouting "Trial by combat" and Donald Trump Jr. streaming "Stand up and fight" Another support of aggressive behavior came from participate Rep. Mo Brooks(R) for Alabama at the rally saying "Taken names and kicking asses" Ben Sassed (R) supported the lies and false trues concerning the election says it was "rigged" and excited the rioters and blood was spilled, using "trial by combat" as Giuliana suggested. The biggest verbal force weighed in was by President Donald Trump spreading the news **"Big Protest in D.C on January 6ᵗʰ be there, will be Wild"**

The domestic terrorist came to the Capitol with molly contrails, pipe bombs, M-4 assault rifles and other dangerous weapons, turning police defense equipment into weapons against the police, using Trump flags to assault the police to bring them down and some were killed. Using the capitol doors as weapons to squeeze the life out of the policemen, what a bang for the 2021 new year for America's Democracy. This aggressive behavior parading itself with confederate flags exciting participates like the Proud Boys, Oath Keepers, White Supremist, Anti-Nazi, QAnons and mobs alike. Their job was to invade and siege the transitional ceremony and the process.

Demonic spirits working inside people's minds, to create a violent siege against Democracy. A Volcano erupting all over this country coming from such right-wing extremist, who has now surfaced to claim their crown of a different America, such as the Bogolo Boys are now out in the open for America to see.

Groups drunk on paraganda and high on radicalism, mind controlling behavior, caught in the moment of despair created by Donald Trump. The incident leaves one to wonder how the rioters demonstrated no cognitive thinking in the chamber room of the Capitol. Some rioters mention "He believed God help them orchestrate this mission, therefore the mobsters went into prayer in the Capitol.

Anger brought them to unexplainable actions, the rioters entering the main chamber room saying "Jesus Christ we can speak your name" verbalizing more to say "Thank your heavenly father that we can stand up to our rights" The domestic mob reflects the reckless brutality against God's people fueled by the actions of President Donald Trump's creating Insurrection through reckless behavior driven by demonic spirits.

A mob fill with limited thinkers, psychologically conditioned by Trump lies, the mob did not think pass their noses. What the rioters didn't realize the grounds of the Capitol is federal jurisdiction, a refuge to a conviction to prison, never the less still doomed by their own actions.

The Mob's action vandalized the Capitol, even Nancy Pelosi

office were a wrecking ball for destruction. Terrorist boldness left Nancy Pelosi a note "We will not back down." The game of chicken President Trump played, has become his cooked duck and his actions has gotten him cooked.

America's Congress had a good taste of Trumps hostel violent hospitality that effected their lives in the Capitol chambers of the Congress on January 6,2021. Domestic terrorist knotting on the front doors of the Capitol with aggressive violent behavior. Carrying weapons of street destruction on the turf of Capitol Hill. Trump supporters put themselves in a position as enemies to Democracy in trying to siege and reject the election, making **"Capitol Hill"** a crime scene for an Insurrection.

America's congress on Wednesday January 6 reaped what Donald Trump soled when he flamed the fire of a violent assault on the Capitol, the People's house. Many cried out that day in prayer such as Rep Grace Merge(D)of New York experienced what prayers means during a crisis, as she called her family from her barricaded room, and they were praying for each other. People seem to know the language to activate God's power when in trouble, but how much spiritual doctrine do people really practice towards personal faith for daily routines.

President Trump had the power to stop the Insurrection by using the Insurrection Act of 1807, a Federal United States law, empowers the president to deploy U.S. military and federal guards in particular circumstances such as a civil disorder, Insurrection and rebellion. President Donald Trump heart was full of vengeance and ignored and refused to activate the Insurrection Act to bring order. President Trump just played it out, like London bridges fallen down and five lives permanently failed, because of this violent civil disorder.

The after mass still left conversations like Ted Cruz greedy for power embedded the false theory of rigged election poisoning the waters with lies, but his actions would not change written America's process. Sen Ted Cruz a traitor to himself demonstrated that he has a clouded mind in accepting the many insults directed towards him and his family from President Trump, during the 2016 presidential race. Ted Cruz still supported president Trump's nonsense of a stolen election.

147 republicans also objected the transfer of power, sore losers who wanted to bully the results. The Republican Red senators could care less who was violated during the Insurrection. These republican senators stuck to their guns, such as Sen. Ted Cruz, Sen Jose Hawley, Sen, Cynthia Lummis. Sen. Roger Mash ell. Rick Scott, Tommy Tourville and Cindy Hyde Smith, all who supports to derail the American vote. The scriptures tell us about these types of characters, noted in Proverbs 29:12 "A ruler hearken to lies, all servants are wicked." This contrast is an example of what's happening in the White House with the Republican Reds.

There is no room for a proud man or woman with lying tongues in God's hands that shed innocent blood "Trump a Dema-god, still processing mind power of the republican party, where 140 republicans supported Donald Trump's against his actions of Insurrection and when the cloud cleared the damaged was done. Trump now well-known of his tactics carries the killer Charles Mansion attitude to control the minds of the republican's base who has become the enemy of Democracy, only because they stand together no matter the circumstances, that may harm the American people.

Vice President Pence a loyal rebel for President Trump and representing the Evangelicals church, is not a goody to-shoe. Vice President Pence speaking out with support for President Trump effort against Democracy was 100%. Vice President Pence spreading false information during press releases to help hold on to their republican party's power.

Mike Pence reckoning is coming for misguiding God's people and pretending to believe in Jesus Christ, his doctrine for humanity but he failed. Mike Pence and the Republican Reds wanted power and complete control of the American people, but they failed!

Vice President Pence grew a conscience, when it came to a demand that he did not believe in, stopping the transfer of the new President Joe Biden. Vice President Pence was considered a traitor in the eyes of President Trump for carrying out his duty in the transfer of changing the guard in reference of a new 2020 president of the United States.

How did these non-patriotic groups form in the first place? Is the light shining on two main characters in Trump's War room? Giuliani and Fleming who some call the Pardon Boys, tattooed by former President Trump's pardons. Trump's war room conversation seemed to spill out the plans for the "Red Wedding" (Insurrection) broadcasting all over social media, signifying the code 1776. what a creative mind, but they say the mind can be a "devil's workshop."

The visual scenes of the Insurrection tell us it was well organized and well-funded. President Trump used electrifying rhetoric to hype up the crowd until shouting occur against Mike Pence saying " **Hang Mike Pence"** A loyal vice president who covered Trump's madness all four years. A man of God who belongs to the Evangelical ministry, has felt his reckoning of bad deeds and demonic spirits has made camp in his life.

Trump was loyal to Pence like Hitler to Stalin during the 1939 cold war in Europe. Hitler and Stalin had a non-aggressive pack that they would not Invade each other but collectively gain power together, but Hitler had other plans. Hitler only used Stalin to buy time and gain economic and military power and later invaded Russia. Trump has no alliance to Mike Pence as Hitler to Stalin, therefore during the Insurrection, were the beginning of Mike Pence, reaping what he sowed by the domestic violence of the mob saying "**Lynch Mike Pence**" remember he was also in the room when the Capital was attacked. Always remember when you take an oath to care for the American people and its Democracy, you must always stay in the right land for humanity, no matter the circumstances. Mike Pence designed his own destiny by not standing for Democracy when Americans needed him most, during the Trump administration. Former vice president Mike Pence writing a book of his repentance called "So help me God" Mike Pence, now asking for mercy from God and the America people who he portrayed.

One big concern about former vice president Mike Pence, his modeling and participation with the Evangelical church Biblical theology. They believe in the preaching of the gospel of Jesus Christ, being born again and retrieving salvation. Administering the authority of the Bible to govern daily living and maintain humanity. The Evangelical church also have invested in universities to teach Christian professionals, how to harmonize careers and spirituality.

Mike Pence and the masses of the Evangelical church supported Donald Trump and his unrighteous actions against standing humanity. Trumps supports individuals from the K.K.K, Proud boys, QAnons, white Supremist and even doctors such as Dr. Stella Emanuel, whose theory focuses on Hydroxychloroquine, as the cure for Covid 19, not masks or shut downs. Dr. Emanuel sees demons having sex with humans as the problem, yet no matter the circle Donald Trump's put himself in, Evangelical church members continue to support President Trump's actions for the "love of money"

What is the real deal at the present time concerning the Evangelical church's organization? According to Franklin Graham CEO of the Evangelical church believes that Donald Trump believes in God, but at the same time Donald Trump's mocks the Evangelical church practices and the laying hands on people for prayer.

Is the Evangelical church driven by money rather than God? Trump advisor an Evangelical participate, received a loan grant from the stimulus package 17.3 million and CEO Franklin Graham received 2 million dollars from the PPl funds. What is wrong with this picture? The Evangelical church is a huge well revenue organization, why would you take money from the people dire need especially during the Pandemic?

To further complicate thinking, Jerry Falwell Jr. president of Liberty University demonstrating unethical actions around women, engaged with sexual acts with his wife and another man. Liberty University has strict conduct codes supporting their belief, but one of their leaders has violated their theology. The question is Jerry Falwell Jr's flesh screaming for sexual activity hidden in the closet of the president of Liberty University? Are these types of behavior a representation of Christianity?

Yet still 66% of the Evangelical organization, supports Trump in his harsh policies and offensive languages, unethical feeling of shaming people of color or who he dislikes and shines light on racist behaviors. American people can be the judge of such behaviors and vote this sickness out of our Democracy only because we must beware of who we interact with as we build strong spiritual practices.

In the book of Revelations, God warns the Ephesus Church concerning the same similar actions as the Evangelical church today. A warning to Ephesus through John's writing of prophecies in the book of Rev. chapter 2 " "Nevertheless I have somewhat against thee, because thou have left thy first love" A warning to correct all churches in the universe to change their behaviors before God comes back. The Evangelical church members who truly love God's theology, now takes the heat for others, who have turn away from the doctrine of Jesus Christ.

The faith to change must be in the eyes of America to endure the dark cloud America is facing today. A demonizing force, President Trump and the Republican Reds twisted and turned the constitution and bill of rights in every way to desperately change America's Democracy to a republican controlled nation with no heart.

On January 13, 2021 president Donald John Trump was Impeached for the 2nd time by the House of Representative for the cause of the Insurrection. The Coronavirus was kinder to Trump than his care for the nation when he survived the Covid 19 and escaped Impeachment.

America needs to take a good look at the Old English nursery rhyme as an example of Trump's behavior as an oppressive leader, like "**Humpy Dumpty** sat on the wall in the 19th English century, Humpy Dumpty had a great fall, all the King's horses and all the King's men couldn't put Humpy Dumpty back together again.

In the rhyme people were dismayed with Humpy, Dumpty dysfunctional behavior, working on the edge, caused him to fall into many pieces, there is no putting him back together. In reality the America people shattered Trump with their American vote and it was over for Humpy, Dumpty Trump.

Americans can defeat whatever is oppressing America like the rhyme of Humpy Dumpy." America is calling on the melting pot who has the tools to help restore the trust to build a bigger, better America back again. Dependable faith keeps hope in your life, builds trust and confidence to create better natural living. Faith is a vision in one's life, that makes you king of the mountain top.

President Donald Trump **"Public enemy number 1"**, the president of the United States has betrayed his country for what the O'Jays often sing about **" For the love of money"** God has bound the hand of Donald Trump and the Republican Reds from any more damage to America's destruction noted in Proverbs 24: 20 For there shall be no reward to the evil man; the candle of the wicked shall be put out"

Trumps idea is to bleed his republican base for money, pretending to start a republican movement for future presidential elections, but really to line his own pockets, remember " money is power." Moving the timeline forward between now and the 2024 primary election will reveal the betrayal of a republican or republicans in Trump's party because other republican seeking presidency too!

A treason act by a republican will be committed against Donald Trump before the 2024 elections. Who will step to the plate or how many will take the chance to find ways to bring Mr. Donald Trump down, so a different Republican can rise to the occasion.

Its breaking news, prophecy is in fresh print and on the wall and it didn't take very long, the timeline has moved into a rolled- over position with movement for change for Donald Trump's life and the republican party. The big wigs, Mike Pence, Greg Abbott and Ron DeSanctis is playing pick-a-boo with Donald Trump for a term of presidency.

Are these men in traitor status like Judas betrayed Jesus for 30 pieces of silver? What price will be payed to betray Donald Trump? Wow, breaking news again for American readers, a rat has brought the cheese to the FBI causing a raid on Donald Trump's dynasty' Mar-a-largo estate for top secret documents. American's top secrets just lying around to become someone else's top-secret talking point, which can allow the enemy to enter the conversation against America's Democracy.

Inquiring minds what to know, will Donald Trump betray his country in time, by exposing America's secrets to others? The demand to return top secret documents were requested by the National Archives in Washington D.C. followed by the Department of Justice to act. The unknown secrets of Donald Trump operations may become known, America stay tuned!

Credit has to be given to God for bounding Trump to stop his mission, the take away for Donald Trump has destroyed the Republican Reds strong hold of political power since 2008. The Republicans has lost the power in the Presidency, House of Representatives, giving the Democrats power to holds the tie breaker held by a Democrat Vice President Kamala Harris all at one time a gift from God.

America must prepare themselves and take a look at the pathways to the Anti-Christ. Trump and the Republican Reds felt their power, with the republican party controlling the senate for over the last 12 years, have started to feel their oats and began a secret movement to become one party and using Democracy to hide behind. Bible history tell us the Anti-Christ will represent the same type of takeover in this same type of fashion republicans are using to form one government. Examples are already set into play, who will rule the world before God's return?

America should pay attention to the Bible and the natural current events all nations are experiencing today. In the pathways to the final Ani-Christ will affect the whole universe, no one will be left out. The Bible mentions this earthly event in Revelations, the Man-God will come from the east. Let's examine who maintains the east.

China is the super power in the east, gaining momentum every day to become the super power of the universe. Where does this put America? outside looking in and has lost its grace and favor from God, noted in Jeremiah 32:33 "And they have turned unto me the back; and not the face: though I taught them, rising up early and teaching them, yet they have hearkened to receive instruction." America will be seized by the Anti-Christ. I know it's a hard pill to swallow but just look at America and their betrayal to the American people by stealing wealth, implementing and operating false conspiracy theories, lies and untrue of reality demonstrated by our leaders who have the power to govern the American people.

Keep looking for the sign are here, measuring the movements of Russia, China, and others, gaining power with other countries to build packs to unite their powers like the B.R.I.S (Brazil, Russia, India, South Africa) or Iran now giving drones to Russia to fight the Ukrainians. Saudi Arabia supporting Russia with oil and snubbing their noses at President Biden and the United States. Countries all over the world are looking to take land from other countries to set up shop of their own methods like China and Russia, who are supporting weaker countries to create better industry and governments, than holding countries at ransom for debt owed, becomes at risk of take over land for none payment of loans.

Fear is in the minds of the people and what will be next on America's agenda, even the fear of Donald Trump coming back to win a presidential race in 2024 may bring on foreign and domestic world Insurrection against the United States, Donald J. Trump has totally lost his mind by denouncing the Constitution saying "A massive fraud of this type and magnitude allows for the termination of all rules, regulations and articles, even found in the Constitution" The cry baby has broken every rule in the book and have tested Democracy, a mega manganic break down and wild behavior, needing mental treatment against himself.

Donald Trump actions will be dealt with by God and he will know it's coming, noted in Proverbs 1:27 "When your fear cometh as desolation and your destruction cometh as a whirlwind, when distress and anguish cometh upon you "This is a clear message. When God gives you leadership over his people, you will have consequences, if you are not set up right. America can clearly see God has bound Trump actions, to do no more in the moment, he has taken his crown. Proverbs 12:22 "The Lord detest lying lips but he delights in people who are trustworthy"

Faith has to be in the eyes of American people in order to create change and be a dominating force. How can we live under the Christian flag and still do awful things to people like crushing a policeman at the Capital between two doors and claim the name of Jesus? How can we look forward to a voice that speaks violence against one another? Faith sprinkles loyalty, a major part of God's theology, you can't flip flop with God, many people see God as a convenience and not a contributor to their belief. In America there are many people, that sends mix messages, causing people to fall away from believing in God.

Donald Trump's actions are an abomination against God, a mockery of the word, noted in Proverbs 6:17-19 "A proud look, a lying tongue, and hands that shed innocent blood", (18)"A heart that deviseth wicked imaginations, feet that be swift in running to mischief,"(19) "A false witness that speaketh lies, and he that soweth discord among brethren.:

Americans demonstrated unbreakable faith against lying tongues, stood the test of time noted in Proverbs 28:5 Evil man understood not judgement; but they that seek the lord, understands all things." Trump and the Republican Reds felt untouchable, concerning their actions and behaviors. Proverb mentions, "An angry man stirred up strife and a furious man abounded in transgression."

It is always important to hold on to correct doctrine and modeling, which affect the way individuals participates in fighting their battles when using spirituality. Studying the word of God is very important, it keeps you correctly sound against any false doctrine. Examining and studying the bible should have the same effort as studying for a certified certificate or college degree, it takes a certain amount of study time to pass the testing to achieve your certification for knowing the scriptures of the living word.

Corrective knowledge is necessary to navigate yourself to healthier living. Look up to God to bring you solutions to turn America's nightmare back into the American dream. There are no real democratic parties only God's party that meets the need of people having no boundaries scene in God's care.

African American Lacey

The African American experience has a past and present history of relic existence of barbarism, torture and death in their first stay in America. White Americans started America's brutal black slavery trade, that became a nightmare for African Americans. A slavery system against African human beings became popular on the shores of Jamestown Virginia near the Atlantic Ocean in 1819.

Americans created the Institution called racism on American soil, documented in every American history book, certifying the institution of black slavery, including Jim Crow laws though white American history shown in the form of white superiority. For decades white American history books, demonstrated critical race theories in their own back yards, where whites controlled how negroes should be viewed in history.

American history is a requirement class for every student receiving a high school diploma in all high schools around the country. How would you feel as an African American student in an American history class, documented you to the only contribution African Americans made were slavery? White American history did give a peep at Sojourner Truth, Harriet Tubman, Rosa Parks, Marcus Garvey, George Washington Carver and Fredrick Douglas and sent African American students on their way to learn more about white historians.

During the slave era there was no justice in site for the African people on American soil and nowhere to run, no matter what southern states black people appear in, if he or she were of African descent, were classified as a slave. During the slave era, white congress representatives' power was depended on how black slaves were counted.

The more slaves you had the more power you had in congress over other states who had less slaves, therefore a compromised became the terms in congress, one slaves would be counted as 3/5th of a person. How can a person be 3/ 5th of a human being? It was all about power and not the souls of human beings

Slavery cursed the African race position here in America, poisoned their minds with the Jimmy Lynch theory. Teaching slaves owners to stop the physical abuse being applied to slaves, but rather condition their minds to enslave themselves to think he or she has no self-worth here in America.

In early history of the African American experience tells us African Americans were not allowed to read and could suffer penalties as hanging. Schools providing poor education to African American children who read from out dated text books, learning subjects 5 years behind, where as white school children receive current text books and informative information to succeed. America demonstrating half-baked education for African Americans, but yet white America still demands that African Americans stand up to white norms with a damaged life. When the Coronavirus hit the nation, it revealed what neigh hoods were outdated and neglected, revealing where money is really spent in what communities.

What America fails to realize, when a child is born, he or she knows very little and cannot talk or walk, children depend on their caretaker where learning takes place. The brain is trained to mature on a continuous base to meet the commands of life. When the mind is restricted, so is knowledge and performance, therefore learning does not take place. America through racism and discrimination limited African Americans potentials for decades, who could have been eligible to be scientists, doctors, politicians,

CEO's, and administrators, just to name a few. America "stop the steal "of Americans lives and put a cap of racism.

Black and brown people are put in designated communities where the revenue is not available for black and brown people to build their communities, but to foreigners who take wealth from Black and Brown communities, where they themselves will not live in, but their business is located there. When will America invest in black and brown people who generations have payed the price to be an American?

Black People were forced to stay segregated, they stepped up to the plate in a city called Greenwood Tulsa, Oklahoma in 1921 over 100 years ago. African American people had created a black wall street for their community. The Greenwood community had been enriched by black doctors, lawyers, bankers, teachers, church leaders, merchants and strong Veteran residents that produced a successful community, because Greenwood Oklahoma was the **Dreamland** out of slavery.

Greenwood was an independent black community with schools, churches and business that host tailor shops, diners, stores, clubs, everything that thrived as a serving community.

A white and black conflict gave whites an opportunity to fuel the fire, for raged white mobs full of hate and murder surfaced and destroy unmercifully, between 100 and 300 African Americans, who were murdered, leaving over 10,000 homeless in the city of Greenwood. Hate reigned all over the mountain top of Greenwood, from white supremist who step in and destroy an African American culture's dream.

White people cloaked in darkness of their sins, tried to erase this massacre off the face of the earth by scattering their bodies under unmarked graves and out of history which created a dark side of silence. This all happen because white people were jealous of what they called African American elite negroes and their families had to be destroyed.

What is the problem with America's conscience and the rule of Law? America has a written document that sets the definition of Democracy and how it's carried out, African American men and women have died protecting America's Democracy. Why does history note that African Americans fought in wars, yet when black soldiers returned home in uniform, still having to sit in the back of the bus or go to the back of the restaurant to buy a cup of coffee why is this?

Noted in the Constitution's 14th amendment states that " All person born, or naturalized in the United States and subject to the jurisdiction therefore all citizens of the United States and of the states wherein they reside". Policies written applies are not enforced. Just like affirmative action had to be added to law in order to delegate fairness especially in the workforce. What happen to the civil right clauses in the Constitution that would have excused affirmative actions. Always remember American Democracy is like a double edge sword it has two systems; one system teaches the norm and the other, America systems policies has been violated and become "weak as water."

Martin Luther King a road runner of civil rights movement and quoted by many, have been violated by America's back tracking to enforce continuous racism all over America, especially towards oppression of black and brown people. Marvin Gaye a visionary revolutionist, expressing himself in song and lyrics, "What's Going On "a prophesy of the present occurrences today and reflecting 50 years ago. Racism and non-equality in our society is still thick as thieves.

Caucasian is a word used to define white culture, Faith is King respects all nationalities in using languages of description, therefore in this glorious nation called America, in the eyes of whites or Caucasians, African Americans have to be twice as good, to get half as much as others. Must be over qualified and always made to feel undervalued. Caucasian Americans never have to wake up and worry about skin color when entering a new job or riding through a Caucasian neighbor to get home.

As long as Caucasian Americans rules, the freedom of African Americans will always have its limitations. Caucasian America progress has been found to depends on the riding of black and brown people to turn the wheels of wealth available to society's chosen few.

From the beginning of America's time Caucasian society has held the flaming touch of racism past down from their generations to their children until this very day, a lot of their children carry the same flame. Where are the pieces to the puzzle of the freedom of an African American man or woman's life, is its still unfinished? will African American people ever have equality in America?

History is repeating its self as America experience another major division. The first major division happen during the time of President Abraham Lincoln. The south left the union refusing to abolish slavery. Slavery became the **Cash Cow** "for the southern states, blacks were producing wealth for everyone but themselves.

During Abraham Lincoln presidential term, he upheld a document acknowledge by the constitution, that in 1865 all slaves would be emancipated. This decision divides the country and the south pulled away from the union which began the "Civil war of blood sweat and tears for many died."

Under slavery African Americans were the engine that maintained revenue to fueling the economic needs of the southern states in the fight to maintain slavery. Another important factor, Lincoln saw that African Americans were the fuel that kept the south competing with the north, causing a delay in winning the war.

President Lincoln orders the freedom of all Slaves in 1865, a document call the Emancipation Proclamation leaving African Americans free with no personal revenue, no stimulus package, just the clothes on their backs for the journey for daily living. The forty acres and a mule for African Americans restitution back in history was just a hex or coup.

Hatred from Caucasian Americans gave African Americans little chance to succeed only looking forward to facing the scars of racism and a brutal history. African Americans wounds are deep and have never healed from that tragic era. Open wounds lie among many, especially the African American people, damaged from the "Civil War" and the horrors of slavery a history that cannot be forgotten.

Racism is a built-in structure involving America's attitude and characteristics, needing total overhaul to address this disease, with change in order to stamp out racism. Today Africans Americans are tired of the smoke screens and promises of having the free will to have the ability to develop an equal life style.

The job to stop systemic racism will be an everlasting fight, racism is a structure embedded in America's fabric and racism will outlast America. African Americans will still have to fight against systemic racism until Christ comes. Let's make it clear again, present day people in power, teach their children to carry that same attitude of superiority their parents embraced. Parents past the Paton of racism to their children who will also looks out the same lens as their parent.

The proof is in the pudding, just look around you and see who still holds the wealth no matter what legislative bills have passed for equal opportunity or what protest is warrant for equal power for others to have a better living already paid for through their individual contribution and revenue taxed based efforts.

To talk about Black Americans is like a merry-go-round, it's like an endless conversation portraying horrifying abuse both mentally and physically against black and brown people. African Americans have scars deeper than the blue sea.

How did America move from the Emmett till execution to George Floyd 9 min execution when republican like Tim Scott says "America is not a racist country? Tim Scott shared on the senate floor about his grandfather experiencing discrimination, that I am sure was a family conversation during that time of high extreme racism. Tim Scott must not have payed attention in high school when teachers taught the American history and the native American experience, where history reveals the racist treatment against native Americans, were created by white Americans and others.

Native Americans worshiped their American land, a symbol of" Mother earth "Why? Because the native Americans treasured the fruits of the land providing all human needs. Here come the foreigners violating their culture, re-arranging infrastructure and rights of land ownership. White Americans killed native American fathers, mothers and children's, then took their land by force and put the native American in designated areas called" **Reservations "on their own land"**

American history also identifies with racism and discrimination through the slaughters of many native American people. Introducing the native American to diseases through medical and drug warfare, accomplishing genocide and oppression leading to native American reservations on their own land. Republican Red Tim Scott needs to wake up and smell the Cappuccino.

Tim Scott has no role models in the US senate but his white Republican Reds, who has taken his courage away to stand up for righteousness for what is needed to serve Democracy. Republican Tim Scott puts on his white face and voted against a champion Ketanji Brown Jackson, an expert in law, and the first over qualified African American women named to judgeship for the highest court in the land "Supreme court of the United States of America ". Tim Scott a traitor to his own culture, blood brother to the Republican Reds and a non-resident of the black community. Regardless why Tim Schott voted "no" for Ketanji Brown Jackson to be supreme court justice, the right people stood up and voted her in to the highest court in the land.

The road for justice has always been a fight for Black Americans, they have seen injustice constantly from visual technology, showing how Black Americans being physically harassed, leading to unlawful beatings and even death, such as Rodney King who experience a terrible inhumane physical beating by Los Angeles policeman. Rodney King's brutal beating was seen by the natural eye and the same injustices still occurs, the policemen set free by the law we are condition to trust.

We can march and protest for the killing of George Floyd, Breanna Taylor, Travon Maritain and many more and still waiting for righteous justice. White America still holding on to racist current events and occurrences of wrongful incidents in the faces of African American people, like in New Hampshire. The handcuffing of a nine-year-old girl, putting her in a squad car handcuffed. while adult male policemen shouting to the nine-year-old" stop acting like a child" and her response "I am a child". The screaming of this child did not make a difference, once she was in the squad car, she was than sprayed by policemen with pepper spray. Racism has been woven in the fabric of America and will almost be impossible to destroy.

The world must know that African Americans have emotional ties to their Black skin color. Blacks have to welcome universal hate where ever they exist, such as the Haitian People a country descended from African slavery. A people who won their independence from France in 1804 now has become one of the poorest Caribbean nation and western hemisphere.

Haitian people reaching out for humanity from others like the United States seeking refuge in Texas from America in 2021 for their horrific pain of calamities and experiencing an assassinated President Juvenile Moise and at the same time experiencing a magnitude 7 hurricanes (Aug 14, 2021) finding much death in the rubble and more poverty. Systematic gang violence, a dysfunctional government and a country seeping into corruption. Tell me who would want to go back to that type of community atmosphere?

America showed no love in the removal of the Haitian people under the Texas bridge. Prodrome on horseback using reins whips to intimidate African Haitians and their children showing no humanity for their condition. America did not even offer vaccines against the killer virus to give them an edge of protection for themselves and others while being be placed elsewhere, even back home to a dying culture.

The most terrifying situation on the Haitian departure, where the shackling, zip ties or handcuffing men and women back home to Haiti, an inhumane tactics. The women who were zipped tied with babies could not even comfort their babies who were crying from a frighten experience on the flight back to Haiti. Ask yourself if this proof of lack of humanity for the Haitian people?

America seemed to turn their backs on Haiti, America should hold some responsible for their welfare. Haiti produces a least 2.5 tons of Calcium Carbonate that makes antacid and aspirin, paint, paper and many other things that make-up 80 percent of their product exported to U.S.A. How does a country remain poor with so many valuable minerals taken from this country being exported all over the world still remain poor?

Racism is a destructive weapon like the Coronavirus, it enslaves life movements of freedom and takes one to the gallows to die. Open your eyes and image being black enslaved in American's racism, never feeling completely freed. The difference between Coronavirus and black people experience is that the vaccine created a relief, but there has never been real relief for African American people in America.

African American's life has suffered much pain today, until it's hard to put into words. Some white people are afraid to identify with truth through words because reading the truth sometimes hurts, when you are that man in the mirror that cannot change. You cannot lump together the painful African American experience and dismiss its hurt because there has been no single defendable aesthetic treatment that is consistent to give a free pass to America concerning the war on African American people.

Today's conversation with whites has been expressed the feeling of their votes have no value, because their white representatives are no longer working for whites but themselves. Let's look at the history of African Americans who had to wait until 1965 to vote, which caused a wave of voter suppression, no faith in the vote and emotional drained for decades to vote among African Americans. The energy among African Americans to vote has improved through education and the fight to maintain freedom.

Racism has transformed itself into segregated mechanism, money not color is now the spark that fuels discrimination against anyone who does not have an abundance of wealth.

According to great historians, black genetics is the D.N.A of life's existence, first man was found in Africa. Noted by genetic historians has arrived and unfolded the continent of Africa seeming about 200,000 years ago scientists called their findings the mother from where all people descended from "Mitochondrial eve"

Americans must stop using African Americans like the Romans

treated the gladiators to win bets among the elite, while the only expectation for gladiators were death. No matter the hoops African Americans jump though or bring basketball to fame, there is a price for a black champion just the same.

How can African Americans stand equal in controlling their lives when they are discredited for taking charge of one's wellness and making healthy decisions. Simone Bibles being discredited by white critics for taking control of her mental wellness. Some speaking out and criticizing Ms. Bibles independence as weak or cowardness. Everyone who understands mental wellness knows the mind controls the body because the brain is your command center.

The most decorated American gymnast raised up coming through the ranks of her grandparents parenting. Grandmother Nellie carried the torch of encouragement and support to her grandchildren's endeavors.

Why does white America always find time to degrade African American champions like Simone Bibles, being the greatest gymnast in the world has achieved over two dozen Olympic and world championship medals. To get to the mountain top was a challenging era, moving from a level 8 gymnast to a junior elite to emerged to senior elite level, being the first African athlete to win all "GOLD" sweeping a championship in the all-around events.

Simone Bibles was not born with a silver spoon, her position was earned by her efforts to achieve. No one talks about Simone's experience to fame along the way, where skin color brings on more trails and tribulation than necessary. In the world of sports, you must be mentally stable and ready for the unexpected, you might be the only one in the room that wakes up knowing you are Black. A young woman dealing with a double-dutch ability to sustain a personal and athletes' life.

Simone Bibles open the door for mental health conversations and actions for others to have that same conversation. Today's well-known celebrities have set their own bounties to preserve and prioritize mental health issues and take a break to re-group.

Mental health authorities need to focus more on mental health and the importance of the brain's operations and its effects on everything we do as human beings. Advancing technologies is overloading the brain to operate under high pressures for daily living, causing mild to chronic mental illness and a breakdown of problem-solving skills for daily functions for the American people, therefore monies must be put back into mental care agencies, a change to avoid an explosion in mental health care.

The Truth about African Americans mental stability, they are gentle giants, making contributions all across world history. Contributions ranging in government, culture, history, literature, art, music, dance and leadership standing. African American history arrives from unconquerable creativity. faith, wisdom and kinship.

There are so many household names contributed to accelerating the African American movements all over the world. African Americans are their own masterpiece in their times and some of the most talented and courageous African Americans pioneers ever lived, in advancing black civil liberty and the rights to equal opportunity to both black and brown people.

It is necessary to acknowledge a gifted young Journalist named Don Lemon coming up in the 21th century to break the barriers in hiding the truth of what happening in the world against God's people. A well needed freedom fighter in the arena of Journalism. A position that can spread the reality of today's Afro American experiences and gather the support needed to stop the fear of the threat from the hooded KKK or White Supremist now in suits and ties from hanging black and brown people's civil rights and liberty.

Don Lemon reaching from his mother and grandmother's wisdom that he embraces as his guiding light in measuring the truth in today's reality. Don Lemon has a fearless attitude, the mouthpiece to reflect what's wrong or right and what we need to do to fix this hidden germ call "racism" that spreads all over the world.

America's timeline has reached the moment, where the truth about African Americans needs to be exposed in all schools where learning takes place. The resistance of white parents coming up with a war on Critical Race Theory to cyanophage what should now be learned about black and white history in all American schools to know the truth about America's collective experience.

The characteristics of Critical Race Theory is the gathering of the minds with civil rights scholars and activist examining race, society and laws and their effects on different races. This type of Knowledge has to have a higher level of education requirement to achieve its understanding, therefore Critical Race Theory area of concentration is taught in higher learning as College. and not the adolescent level, therefore why rally around the flag creating chaos but instead create the conversation for all to get-a-long.

American black experience will be an endless conversation. Generations after generations have fought the same battles of their forefathers concerning systematic racism, which has always been in the front row of African American lives, having a tortured soul that will never go away. Always remember knowledge is power and *Ignorance is bondage.* The most important message to be found for the spirit of African American men and women is the conversation of true freedom Noted in John 8:36 " If the son therefore shall make you freely, shall be free indeed." God's, freedom is does not cost you anything, especially your life.

AMeRiCa's BROKeN VesseL

Joe Biden loves his country and came forth for a Job he knew he must do, to restore Democracy in America, taking the challenge in running for president against an alien seated as an Autocrat, President Donald Trump has become "Enemy in Democracy's camp"

Senator, Vice President Joe Biden has been in the political arena for over 40 years, a long-term believer in the power of the legislator. A humanitarian, long term economic growth organizer. Vice President Biden spent 8 years working with President Obama, history being made.

During Both terms President Obama and Vice President Joe Biden experienced first hands in working with a racist and discriminatory administration, who deliberately rejected President Obama's presidential services because of the color of his skin, with no chances of the senate who held the deciding power to cooperate during the terms of President Obama and Vice President Biden.

Vice president Biden being second in command with President Obama but first by color had an experience of walking in the shoes of a black man. Today those experiences put President Biden wisdom in the front row in leadership and the fight to bring back Democracy.

Former Vice President Biden knows what tools to use in restoring and building back a better America. A leadership edge to create a stronger foundation that is unbreakable among the American people, developing a well diverse unified plan of operation to rebuild the broken parts of America.

When God approves you of a task to be achieved he will empower you, as Biden is a master of his professional administration, God knows Biden understands the job he is facing, noted in II Timothy 2:24 " And the servant of the lord, must not strive but be gentle unto all men, apt to teach" this is Joe Biden a great man of character in every form and fashion especially at home with his family, who he loves dearly. A national political leader, Joe Biden molded by ordinary hard-working people, who's family ethnics developed a platform of righteous family values, which work to created opportunity for healthy living and forward achievement in the Biden's family.

God has been good to Vice president Biden during his life time tragedies, because of his faith Noted in Psalms 145:9 The Lord is good to all; and his tender mercies are over all his works. As the song writers wrote" what a man, what a man, what a mighty good man"

God blessed Joe Biden in the time of family needs, with a special woman of love. God gave him back a strong new family which included Jill Biden, who brought love to help balance the family's strength for healthier living. Jill Biden humble enough to become a part of the family tree, to help with growth, healing and carry the family obstacles they faced in their lives determined to turn life around.

Vice president Joe Biden is a moderate man and a great problem solver, demonstrating his skills like a warrior in the story of David and Goliath fighting an enormous giant. President Biden knows his craft and has the patience of "Job" (A biblical historian) who out lasted Satan's wish to conquer his faith away from God, who he loves so dearly.

The 2021 presidential Inauguration of Joe Biden, where the red carpet was finally rolled out for vice president Joe Biden, the next President of the United States of America. Our celebration should further extend the celebration for our Lord Jesus Christ, the one who made this day happen.

Grace from God shut down Donald Trump, change the gate

keeper and restored his best servant Joe Biden. Without God there would have been no exchange, but change came by the prayer counted sent up to heaven to change the gate keeper during these trying times of a Demigod behavior, former President Donald Trump.

The Day finally came for Inauguration for the presidential transfer on January 20 2021, America's Democracy rose and stood up, choosing President Biden and Vice President Kamala Harris to lead the country. In our visual sight the world saw witness to senator vice president Biden and senator Harris putting their hand on an extortionary Book, "The Bible" to take their oath for presidential offices. This is a prime example of the tools we used for legal engagement and the reason we must hold true and increase representing our spirituality in our communities.

American people have spoken and their actions completed on Inauguration day to continue to build a more perfect union. President Joe Biden and Vice president Kamala Harris accepting their position to help govern the United States of America and America's foreign affairs.

A new President Biden has identified the condition of America and has pledge a wartime strategy to get America back on track. Recognizing America's most important fight, the Coronavirus and the many unknown pathogens on America's territory. Medical scientist seeking refuge to get back to normal and return home, ending the epidemic nightmare. In order to get back to normal, America must travel the avenues of medical science to control and conquer the Coronavirus that causing economic strife, poor health care, racial unrest, systemic racism and a nation in division only "**Unity**" can fix.

President Joe Biden who carries a spiritual attitude, humbling himself to Donald Trump Narcissistic behavior. President Joe Biden knows how to respond to his opponent noted in Proverbs 16:19 "Better it is to be of humble spirit with the lowly, then to divide the spoils." When you know what is expected in your spiritual belief than you will accomplish your goals in a Godly way because, noted in Proverbs 17:20 "Better he that handled a matter wisely shall find God and whoso trusted in the Lord, happy is he"

President Biden knows where his strength lies and he walks with a spiritual attitude. Joe Biden is known to embrace individuals who have faced tragedies and unfavorable occurrences in their lives. President Biden having tragedies in his own life, still extending strength and kindness to many families who also faced tragic in their lives. The good and faithful servant still used tones of love to help others heal in their own experiences, in Psalms 145:20 notes" The Lord preserveth all them that love him: but all the wicked will he destroy".

Forgiveness is power, staying focus on what makes the world go around, eliminating demonic measure and strife to peaceful movement in what's right for all. President Biden knows he has an uphill battle to heal Democracy, even though he knows he inherited Trump's dirty laundry, blamed for everything Trump left behind.

President Biden had to stop Trump's parade and the Republican Reds from spreading an embedded disease-causing Americans to be demonized away from Democracy and at the same time holding on to the Affordable Care Act that covers over 21 million people in America, so desperately needed especially during the Pandemic.

President Biden will fight the cloud that brought American 's darkness, the brutal fight against negative forces trying to interfere in God's decision that he has changed the "**Gate keeper.**" **Noted in Psalms 75:7 " But God is the judge, he putted down one, and setteh up another "President Joe Biden in charge, the new gate-keeper under God's command and the People's vote.**

The power of acceptance for President Biden, noted in Jeremiah 1:10 "See I have this day set thee over the nations and over the Kingdom, to root out, and to pull down, and to destroy and to throw down, to build, and to replant. God will even hasten his word to be seen all over the world, where gates are strengthened by the power of his word. Always remember God takes pride in his people and will see them through, therefore praise God for his promise, we must sound our trumpets for the free world, which has returned to the people by the people. The American people clanged onto their **Democracy** with the only power they could depend on "their **Vote**."

America is in a crucial period and needs a treatment plan to repair America's foundation. President Biden, Vice President Kamala Harris and the democratic administration plan must cover a metaphysical and medical restoration, a big dose of faith that brings healing and relief from suppression of Donald Trump and the Republican Red Party.

President Biden has picked the very best official presidential cabinet in the nation. Remarkable Americans bringing their stories and roles of expertise and honor to the table as a public servant. Biden has also asked Americans to give him time to jump start the administration to bring resolutions to American Democracy that was almost destroyed.

The Biden Administration can build back better in areas of economics, Infrastructure, health care, family care, Immigration and job advancements with higher wages. The real emergency todays should mainly focus on helping the American people get the relief needed during this critical time. American is experiencing the Pandemic's after mask under the new administration. Nina Simone singing lyrics " It's a new dawn, a new day and I am feeling good" lets feel good America.

America's economic relief is in shadows of pain, but President Biden stands by saying "Help is on the way", Biden will be the light in darkness of America. President Biden was given his post as president of the United States of America, by the American people and the almighty God.

President Biden and his administration will need a holistic approach to rebuild a broken vessel here in America. Emotional rebuilding will also be needed, the confidence and trust that builds empires. President Biden efforts is to restore and repair America's broken vessel.

In August 2022 President Biden roaring like a Lion instead of a kitten, speaks out with thunder in his voice, in campaigning for the

2022 democratic primary. President Biden today spoke to America as a true general of Democracy, pointing out "Extremist Trump and the mega republicans did nothing to help the American people get back on their feet. The only thing the mega republicans brought to the table were a blank agenda, viciousness, anger, hate and division, well spoken by President Biden.

President Biden also mentions that the mega republicans demonstrated non-support of the bills needed passing to advance Americans out of their dilemma. The mega republican's extreme ideology must be dismissed in order to continue down the road to repairing and to move forward with unity, hope, attitude of optimism and our Democracy!

The light is shining in President Biden's favor, his wisdom is leading the way, his accomplishments are climbing the mountain where the weather is ice cold in getting the republicans on board to rid the ice storm and the restoration that America so desperately echoing.

President Biden proved to the American people the best way to America's resolution is "bipartisanship", his accomplishments has rung the bell in a $1.2 trillion bipartisan infrastructure package, $1.9 trillion Covid relief deal, demonstrated having the highest number (73) in appointment for federal judges, Halt on executions, reduction in unemployment, passed the Chips act, Pack act for veterans and the biggest package in decades is the inflation reduction act, which includes revenue tax reform, lower prescription drugs, climate restoration, energy improvements and more.

President Biden has not given up on what he came to do for Democracy, he has "walk the walk and talk the talk for better days ahead. We truly can recognize his battle and his faith, noted Galatians 6:9 And let us not grow weary of doing good, for in due season we will reap, if we do not give up "If America holds up as Sam Cook sings, a change is coming!

TRUTH BRINGS TRUST

Time is rapidly changing to meet the demands of the new world order in technology. This new world order is called Artificial Intelligence an idealist way of living. Artificial Intelligence is a money-making device that has reached all over the world. The use of Artificial Intelligence has driven our authoritarian powers to the point of greed with no humanity insight.

Americans must pay attention, not to become an artificial robot or allow mind controlling chips to be placed in our brain that shows no empathy for humanity. Do our minds collect the right data and send out false messages, to benefit self, regardless if decisions trample over others?

America has allowed aliens, domestic and foreign adversaries to surface to filtrate our Democracy. During Trump's administration America has experienced a government leaning towards an authoritarian dictatorship, the same time America is having whirlwinds of dramatic catastrophes in and around the world.

If America becomes an authoritarian, autocratic monopolized government with the help of Artificial Intelligence, Democracy will disappear. The American people will have little or no chance to make their own choice of healthy living and investment prosperity. Instead the essential workers will continue to build the wealthy's life style with little return.

The unidentified wealthy in America is now in charge, the

average person who identities with this type of wealth, start feeling their own power and wealth becomes their God in worship. The greed of men and women today will not share their wealth with anyone. Noted in Psalms 115:4 "Their Idols are **silver and gold** the work of men's hand."

The wealthy and big businesses who profile their agenda towards greed, have no problem riding the backs and taxing hard-working people, where the large corporations connected to family and friends, pay little or no taxes and raise the cost of living beyond reach for most Americans, where only the wealthy lavish life styles are being honored.

The wealthy investors count on the lower waging Americans to spends their earnings to gain much profit. Poverty keeps the economy moving, Industries producing products centered around working-class consumer's needs for living. A supply and demand concept that make people rich, an example of this message is shown, when America failed to its economy during the 2020 Coronavirus, rich investors became wealthier, while the people on the ground experienced horrible losses.

The role of America's Industry is not loyal to the American people, but reflects their energy towards wealth such as Dow futures, NASDA future and S&P 500. America's wealth authorities are only interest in ranking among the wealthy that brings world powers. Wealthy Gurus have given American people and their families a good wake-up call and where their allegiance stands.

Some men and women want to destroy and replace the very thing this country was once built upon. Truth and Trust in our society is disappearing and replaced with lies that create smoke screens causing Americans to live in the dark along with the rest of the World, it's a worldly thing. We cannot afford today not to trust our leaders who make decisions on our behalf, the real truth brings trust that affects one's existence.

In the last days of President Trump and his republican party's control, they conditioned the American people to operate on lies and broken trues. American government operated on lies as truth, a new norm for the American people. Fanning the flames of misinformation results in untruths and no trust between one another and the nation.

High risk of failure is certainly involved when using wrongful avenues to gain wealth against humanity's orbit. Noted in Matthew 17:26"For what is a man's profited, if he shall gain the whole world, and lose his own soul? or what shall a man give in exchange for his soul? To worship money does not last, money cannot save America experiencing out of control calamities. Calamities that leads to death, and unrepairable destructions allowed and controlled my God because of disobedience against mankind.

The middle-class essential workers of America along with the unfortunate class, have lost their faith and trust in America. Hard working people, left out of the equation of having a piece of the American's dream. The truth that effect our lives has become clouded, therefore we must search deeper, become explorers, seeking and discovering truths from a force stronger than man, woman and child.

IN 2020 Sunday, vertical services supported what America and the world needs for change. Bishop Lampert Gates Jr of Kingdom Apostolic ministries in 2020 on a wintery Sunday, began his vertical message with a topic, "Looking for a change." This message expresses that change comes under preserving God's house necessary to be used as a central network to let the Holy spirit be the changer and balance in your life, therefore allowing you to make the transformation during the storms in one's life.

Our conversation among Americans has to consist of implementing truth back into the American dream. Truth is the rock to build upon, noted in Deuteronomy 32:4 "He is my rock, his work is perfect for all his ways are judgement; a God of truth and without iniquity, just and right is he". Truth is the only thing in building your own personal portfolio to stand upon, noted in John 3:18 " Dear children let us not love with words or speech but with actions and "Truth."

Trust is assimilated with truth, truth should be your heart beat to maintain trust. Trust holds its own standard it's not a word designed to kick around, if you mishandle the word trust, it will lose its value.

You cannot get the true value of trust if you violate its meaning. Trust involves many true characters, covering honesty, straight forwardness, strength, confidence, reliance, integrity, communication and loyalty to your purpose. Most of all trust builds bonds between one another.

Broken trust shows false images of yourself, this becomes a real problem especially when you have a person in authority, responsible for governing a people, but your platform consist of broken promises, lies, violating the expectation of the people, avoiding problem solving and lack communication among the people. A prime example of a person demonstrating mis-trust is Hershel Walker running for the 2022 midterm election to represent the Georgians in congress. Hershel Walker trying to win a senate seat, but comes with baggage of deceit, lies, no ethnic bounties and zero experience.

The bible speaks that men and women would honor wrong things of life, noted in Isaiah 5:20 " Woe unto them that put darkness for light and light for darkness; that put bitter for sweet; sweet for bitter" to deny a good man's steps like senator Warlock noted in Isaiah 5:23 "Which justify the wicked for reward and take away the righteousness of the righteous." Scriptures tell us what man will do, therefore do what you know best. Use your vote to keep life right and senator Warlock with a victory!

An old time saying " "Your word is your bond, a badge of honor, therefore you must demonstrate truth in your voice when you speak, your speech should reflect your actions. America has to go back to being honest, an old American saying "Honesty is the best policy" supported by ll Corinthians 18:5 " For we can do nothing against the Truth, but for the Truth".

America has been beaten down to the point the average person suffers from mistrusting anybody but themselves. Fighting with America political parties is not what we need to reset and build back to gain an American unified front. Utilizing collective facial knowledge and manpower together can build a proactive infrastructure that works for every American's family. Noted in Proverb 24:14 " So shall the knowledge of wisdom be unto thy soul; when thou hast found it, then there shall be a reward, and thy expectation shall not be cut off" always remember your supports comes from scriptures of the "Good Book."

Americans must stay the course being proactive with the truth about our realities in America and how it affects our lives. American families need to be healthy, both mentally and physically to manage healthy living.

American people have a challenge in order to build back trust that bonds one another to maintain healthy living through choices of your own. Our backs have been ridden on long enough, the time has come to say" enough is enough "make a strong stand and position ourselves with the right values of humanity, taking the pathways back to unifying our American dream and the constitution we should live by.

We must strengthen and empower back our families in America, the central core where Gods implements unity through family participation and application. A family is a wonderful partnership with people you love and trust. Your family is the greatest support system, the nucleus of human existence, the center of where we can from. We must never hide the truth from our children, children need to live in a world of reality, making changes along the way for a positive future.

Families have many different strengths to help you build along the way, starting with extended families consisting of grandparents, aunts, uncles and cousins living close by.

There are a variety of strong family foundation in developing family structure such as morals, customs, traditions, and values. Ensuring teaching values that makes children stand strong and endure the challenges of life. Good family characteristics such as social skills, spirituality, morality, values, economical readiness and good health.

The greatest learning experiences starts at home, where families are responsible for a child's primary learning environment. Parents play a significant role in early childhood development until adulthood, where the course is set in teaching the norms of society.

Educational enhancement should also be a key for learning during childhood experiences, which helps children make a smoother transition into adulthood. Families modeling good characteristics both mentally and physically creates sound healthy living.

The lack of good child development through parenting keeps children's mindset limited, causing childhood behaviors to spill over into adulthood. This child like behaviors keeps adults in a frame mind of making childlike decision, but held responsible to be an adult.

The truth that effect our lives has become clouded but repairable, you must prepare yourself and seek to change your position, this is your second change to rise. We must now turn towards the original creator, when God gave man free will, he did not expect man to separate himself from the principles and true theology of God's living word.

Adding spirituality to your life holds you tighter, when there are no immediate answers. Faith is King messages will cover the knowledge of the truth, who is responsible for our universe and where should our focus be?

The real focus should be creating healthy personal portfolios to perpetuate growth is the answer, family enrichment, financial foundations, higher learning and character building is a target for advancement. Learning to increase your spirituality through faith and beliefs works towards being a powerful Christian too.

We must find faith in a new theology, (Theo- means God) logy means (the study of) in Greek. Theology is a systematically developed study of spiritual beliefs. It examines the human experience of faith and how different people express and respond. Theology examines the structures to better understand the philosophy and the experiences behind it. God 's theology provides doctrines through scriptures examining his principles with teaching instructions.

We are all righteous in the eyes of Jesus who died on the cross in his own blood. Yet we know that a person is made right with God by faith in Jesus Christ. You don't have to have man's approval to feel righteous, the question will be, do you want to be righteous?

The objective of God's grace is to demonstrate wholesome living and be right in the eyes of God by faith. Let God pilot your directions in life and be your driver. Man's biggest mistake, he wants to succeed on his own efforts and be like God without God, remember we have choices.

God has empowered man and women to take a duel role in building a productive personal portfolio for healthy living. The task will be learning how to live a natural life and a spiritual life at the same time. The spiritual role has more dominion over natural roles because Gods theology reflects his power that involves dominion over the world. (Palms 24:1) The earth is the lord's and fullness thereof: the world and to they that dwell there in. All you need is clarity about Jesus Christ and you will be on your first step to seeking righteous living.

In our travel to learn more about God, you will find that God can operate through natural occurrences in our lives to inform, warn, guide and judge. God's main strategy is to help individuals maintain divine order in their lives. This is the main reason God gave men and women free will with a certain amount of power to govern their lives righteously. No matter what time in time, men and women have changed their hearts to fit their own personal needs without sharing with others, this has become the norm in America and all over world.

SPiRiTuaL CORNeRSTONeS

Spiritual investment in life's security comes from **belief, faith, worship and prayer,** a successful spiritual foundation. This structured formula **belief, faith, worship and prayer** has to be embraced, implemented and applied to daily living. Belief is trusting, faith is loyalty, worship is application, and prayer is your personal conversation with God, a petition of promises through believing and building close relationships with God.

Belief is the first step to helping you identify your faith, in something that is true and exist. If you look at the word belief in a spiritual context, belief is described as having a confident attitude towards God, which involves commitment and faith in holy theology. Most people believe there is a higher power, people feel safer saying there is a higher power without making a psychological commitment to participate in the atmosphere of spirituality.

Faith is a tool for building permanent healthy living through confidence, trust, assurance in what you hope for. A pledge to your own well-being, demonstrated through devotion and participation. Faith is a way to take a stand in what you believe in. Noted in Hebrews 11:6 "But without faith, it is impossible to please him; for he that cometh to God must believe that he is, and that he is a rewarder of them that diligently seek him.

Faith must be practiced to establish hope, without hope noted in Proverbs 13:12 "Hope deferred maketh the heart sick: but when the desire cometh, it is the tree of life." Unbreakable faith has been exhibited by many individuals in biblical history and the present. It is important that you take a stand in representing your unbreakable faith.

Unbreakable faith

Unbreakable faith must be a strong hold in your life, it starts with walking and speaking the truth. Shinning your light brings good fruit, remember demonstrating righteousness comes with a price, therefore to reach this goal, you must have the proper equipment to battle the things in life. Ephesians 6:11 "Put on the full armor of God so that you can stand against the tactics of the devil"

No matter what battles you are facing your pledge with God has to be known as an unbreakable chain. Biblical history has shown us examples, how the importance of soldiering up. Let's take a good look at the story **of David and Goliath,** a giant standing six cubits and a span tall (9ft 9 inches), fully armed with brass, holding a sword weighting six-hundred shekels of iron, Goliath size was defiantly a threat to the Israelites, the fight between the two was over territorial bounties whereas, whoever wins the battle takes rule and Saul the King, was afraid of the outcome of the battle between David and Goliath.

David was not afraid, he had an unbreakable pledge with God and took the challenge of Goliath. David with a weapon of 5 smooth stones and his sling shot apparatus, defeated the giant by hitting him square in his forehead dropping him for the kill, then cutting off his head with Goliath own sword. Psalms 56:22 "Cast thy burdens upon the Lord, and shall sustain thee; he shall never suffer the righteous to be moved" With the words of God teaching provided guidance for David where he knew he was protected by his God in this battle he conquered.

Shadrack, Meshach and Abednego were also tested concerning their unbreakable pledge to God in the time when King Nebuchadnezzar had made a huge golden image like God for his people and nations to bow down to an image of a false God.

The decree was made by the King for his people, when the people heard the sounds of different instruments playing all types of music, would be the time to bow down to the golden Image as if it was a God or be put in the fiery furnace.

Sharrock, Meshach and Abednego refused because Jesus was their God. This made the King full of fury, demanding that the furnace be heated up 7 times higher than normal. The 3 brothers were bound and thrown in the fire, and even the men who open the doors to the furnace were burned to death.

The fiery furnace became hot as hell, the King looks in and what does he see? a fourth man walking with the 3 brothers unharmed from the blazing fire, Jesus keeping his promise to protect his own.

This last Biblical cornerstone involved a man called **Daniel,** who loved his God dearly, took time aside to pray every day. Daniel was a true and faithful servant to the king and well respected by him, this granted Daniel favor.

Jealousy can be your worst enemy, other Kingsman disliked Daniel and betrayed him. The kinsmen claiming to the king that Daniel did not consider the king his God and prayed to another. The rule in the kingdom, if anyone does not regard the king as a God would be put in the Lion's den.

Daniel was taken by the King's order to the Lion's den, surrounding him with the king of the jungle, Daniel would be eaten alive., but the king did not realize, God is also king over the lions in the jungle, remember God is king over all things in the universe. When Daniel was looked upon in the Lion's den, they saw the Lion's mouths were shut tighter than a hat band. Daniel knew his unbreakable pledge to serve the lord would ignite God's promise to protect him.

John Lewis a great man of unbreakable faith, a teacher of wisdom determined to teach others in finding a path to righteous purpose. John Lewis born February 21, 1940 becoming a young African American advocate for human rights, determined to keep the door open for a continuous fight for equal civil human rights for African Americans and others.

John Lewis at the age of 25 took yet another challenge, a challenge that almost cost his life. On Sunday March 7, 1965 marching towards the Edmund Pelts Bridge in Selma Ala, named after confederate general and grand dragon of the K.K.K. John Lewis was first to be beaten almost to his death by state troopers, leaving him with a bloody cracked skull. Followed by a bloody trail of participates, so bloody until they called that day "Bloody Sunday."

John Lewis continued pushing his way, teaching and guiding to open doors to justice, all the way to the House of Representatives. An American statement and civil rights leader, shouting words of wisdom to never lose your direction or focus in the fight for human rights for all.

John Lewis last walk was supporting Black Lives Matter movement, fighting against murdering and killing of black and brown people. John Lewis work added a stain of good measure believing "Get in good trouble, necessary trouble " State representative John Lewis final day came on July 17, 2020 a celebration of his legacy left behind.

President Barack Obama, spokesman at John Lewis's ecology at Ebenezer Baptist church the home of Martin Luther King in Atlanta, Georgia. President Obama describing John Lewis as a great civil rights Icon, to be crowned of his glory as a gladiator on the battlefield expressing righteousness. Praises also came from people in high places, trail blazers, blazing the trail for Democracy on John Lewis homecoming were former President Clinton and former President Brush giving their last respect to an honorable man.

Barack Obama last words at John Lewis's ecology, sighting a similarity of Johns Lewis and Paul (a Biblical historian) noted in Act 18:9-10 "Than spoke the Lord to Paul in the night by a vision, be not afraid, but speak, and hold not thy peace for I am with thee, and no man shall set on thee to hurt thee: I have much people in this city" when we have faith in our hearts using Holy words to support our mission around the world, it's our petition to God. Noted in Psalms 66:19 "But very God hath heard me, he hath attended to voice of my prayer."

John Lewis knew the American people were still struggling with being oppressed especially during the Pandemic, he knew his words must stand strong in support of America's pain during America's Coronavirus life, expressing that "We might be struck down but not destroyed, we can make this country reach it highest potential" calling on the American people to redeem faith and liberate the soul to truth. The testing of Americans faith becomes a service to unify in building back a bigger better America with unified support of all-American people.

One important thing to always remember, you must note, that Christian Americans carry their spirituality on their sleeves. Always marching for protection against unrighteous and fighting battles of oppression and discrimination everywhere Christians go. Christians do not identify with color but a belief to demonstrate rightful living.

Muhammad Ali one of the greatest boxers in the world, in his time stood alone, no Black Lives Matter organization marching for the rights of Muhammad Ali, but Ali's unbreakable faith. With a loud strong voice, he demonstrated being a beautiful black unmovable movement, his skin color was wrong but the money was right for whites in the boxing enterprise.

Champions are born through family traits, character development and encouraging atmospheres, that's make a true champion. Muhammad Ali had no shelter, standing alone to systemic racism in every step he took, at any time Muhammad Ali could be in violation in the eyes of whites, because of his skin color, even Jim crow laws stay in his face and around every corner spying on his every movement. In Muhammad Ali time, whites ignite hatred even when it was unnecessary.

Muhammad Ali was a great man, he knew where his strength and guidance came from noted in Psalms 27:2 "**THE STEPS** of a good man is ordered by the Lord; and he delighted in his way". God gave him the intelligence and skills to guide his way into being the greatest fighter in the world of boxing using his intellectual mind and his mighty fist.

Muhammad Ali had unbreakable faith for himself, family and profession. His greatness in the sports of boxing was untouchable, his impact in representing black people was imaginable, every punch he threw black people threw, having the feeling of joy seeing a black boxing champ in the ring, at the same time black people were fighting against the feeling of systemic racism.

When Muhammad Ali came out the corner with his fancy footwork and his mighty blows, African American people in the moment came out that same corner, imaging themselves hitting white people through Ali 's punches to get back at whites for their horrible treatment and brutal behavior against black and brown people. Through the strength of Mohammad Ali punches, black people were winners for the moment knowing that equal freedom and opportunity was still far away.

Professional fighter Icon Muhammad Ali kept self-pride alive through all his pain he was still a great Afro American citizen, woven in his character as he demanded respect as a black human being. A great African American traveled down a highly professional athletics path, in a role with no voice among whites, but he felt his own voice was good enough because faith was unbreakable and he became the world **Champion** in the sport of boxing.

Another brother **Colin Kaenick** standing alone for justice, while his comrades who shared the same activities, petted him on his back, to say "You're doing the right thing," but few participated in the support of his cause called " Justice". Others being too afraid to lose their position and lavish life styles, but those same brothers who were afraid to stand up also have been victimized going home from the sport arena by racist individuals too!

Always remember, there is power in kneeling especially in protest against threats of racism for black Americans all over the world no matter how talented you are. Sometimes when authorities refuse to do and be right, kneeling support's calling for change from a power greater than man or woman. Noted in Ephesian 3:14 " For this because I bow my knee unto the father of our Lord Jesus Christ." Knowing the only dependable change comes from God. There is no violation here when you ask for change from a power greater than man.

Black professional athletes are waking up for a stand of faith in believing that Black lives matter, not careers this time. Professionals rallied around unbreakable faith for change, step in on the death of George Floyd, Breonna Taylor, Trayvon Martin, Michael Brown and the shooting of Jacob Blakes, shot in the back 5 times in front of his boys, where is the change for the value of African American lives?

The deaths and tragedies have broken the camel's back and sparked special attention of Black Lives Matter organization. The cries of sorrow rings into the atmosphere, as the death angle awaits. The cries for help effected Labron James emotions and he reacted, rallying with the NBA, WBA, Tennis professionals, college athletics and many more, all to say enough is enough and black lives matter too!

How does it feel to play professional sports and be a famous Icons and still have no voice with the people you make all the money for? Eleanor Roosevelt says "You must do the things you think you cannot do" And from the efforts of professional athletics speaking caused a rippling effect of negotiating the use of Sports Arenas as an effort for more comfortable voting polls for the people voting in the presidential election in 2020. Don't stop your acknowledgement of power you have, you have more power than you think in your walk for humanity.

MS Yvonne Stacey Abrams also leads with unbreakable faith, an American politician, lawyer, voting rights advocate and founder of "Fair Fight." Stacey Abrams with high profile credentials, serving in Georgia House of Representatives and a minority leader. Stacey Abrams, who lost the race for Governor of Georgia in 2018, marred by allegations of voter suppression.

Stacey Abrams defeat only looked for victory ahead as she soldiered-up, climbing into the trenches, setting up strategic plans to help Georgians empower themselves with their votes for better representation to reflect their own communities for their needs and care. Fair quality systems have to be in place in all voting operations and to assure there is equality in the decisions that will impact our lives through our vote.

Stacey Abrams a magnificent trail brazier in clearing the path against the sink holes of suppressive elections used to defeat her in the running for governor in Atlanta Georgia. Stacey Abram knew she still had a job to do, now a messenger and leader for strategic planning that clears the way for honest voting opportunity offered to all Georgians. Stacey Abrams stands with Biblical expression of symbolic bravery noted in Proverbs 30:30 "A lion which is strongest among beast, and turned not away for any." Stacey Abrams roaring effects are shared with many who has created movements to show Americans the power is in your vote!

Stacy Abrams efforts along with other cultural voters turned Georgia into a blue state held my Republican Reds for over 8 years. Demographics and investment groups changing their landscape of Georgians to build a better America for all Americans.

A magnificent effort shown by Ms. Abrams, during the 2020 Presidential election in Georgia, turned Georgia into a Blue State. Electing Joe Biden as democratic President of The United States of America, an end to Trump and the Republican Reds supremacy. Stacey Yvonne Abram did not win govern ship in 2022 mid-term election, but still Stacy Adams is a champion born to lead in the land of Democracy.

Unbreakable faith creates wisdom articulated from time spent in your belief, worship and prayer, it's the round-up for building a spiritual lifestyle. Under the umbrella of change wisdom is an unbreakable tool to developed through experience and knowledge gained as maturity sets in life's timeline.

Wisdom used properly can assure better healthy living as you participate with your family and community. Gandhi says "Be the change you wish to see in the world. "Wisdom gives you the ability to be that change, to think and develop maturity in better decision making in one's life. Wisdom certifies you in having good critical thinking, unbiased judgement and experienced maturity.

In higher heights of learning, you must take along wisdom, it is knowing the quality of knowledge and its benefits. Experiences gives you the direction to good judgement. Noted in Proverbs 2:6 "For the Lord gives wisdom, from his mouth comes knowledge and understanding.

Wisdom leads you in the path of righteous behavior noted in Biblical history "Wisdom is before him that hath understanding; but the eyes of a fool are is the ends of the earth. Wisdom is a tool God gives us to use in decision making and how we can privatize our life through faith.

Biblical history has also given us a perfect example of the power of wisdom with King Solomon, the youngest King in Biblical times. God appeared in a dream noted in 1 King 3:5 "In Gibeon the Lord appeared to Solomon in a dream by night; and God said" Ask in what I shall give thee" King Solomon recognizing that he was a child with a man's responsibility to governor God's people. Solomon asking noted 1 Kings 3:9 " Give therefore thy servant an understanding heart to judge the people that I may discern between good and bad.; for who is able to judge this thy so great a people" God was pleased with King Solomon and his ways, that he was a faithful servant. King Solomon was also chosen by God to be the first King to build God's magnificent temple.

The Bible speaks more clearly "Wisdom is before him that hath understanding; but the eyes of a fool are in the ends of the earth. "He that getter wisdom loveth his own soul; he that keepth understanding shall find good. There is nothing wrong about feeling good about self. Wisdom accelerates with time and growth, wisdom is a perfect tool to guide you in healthy living. Noted in 19:8 " The one who gets wisdom loves life, the one who cherishes understanding will soon prosper.

Worship

Worship is a lifestyle representing your beliefs, surrendering yourself to take on the ways of God's holiness and still hold on to your free will, to make plans and decisions in your life for a natural spiritual healthier living.

You cannot worship God with ignorance, because the devil is intelligent, to avoid the power of Satan in your life you must have

Biblical knowledge. A continuous participation to read the scriptures is necessary to guide you and assist you with daily living especially on the problem-solving part of your life.

Successful worship feeds off on how much time spent through participation and commitment to what you believe. Spirituality can create major positive productivity in your life. Primary focus on commitment and participation is needed in learning the importance of worship. The acceptance of God's Holy theology puts you in a state of mind to cognitively believe in developing your degree of faith in the purpose of worship.

The important message here is to allow God to be in charge of our lives guided by God's play book (Bible). God gave men and women the earth to provide themselves with healthy living, not destroy the earth with greedy tactics in mind that causes destruction. God provides us with all provisions to live and enjoy life in the right way.

Involving yourself with God, celebrates worship, enjoying and showing strong arbitration for humanity. (Roman 1:6)"For I am not ashamed of the gospels of Christ for it is the power of God unto salvation to everyone that believeth"

Worship demonstrates love expressions heard in our voices through music, praises, speeches, word reading, prayer, love and fellowship. In your worship comes testimonies that tell stories of real-life experiences. Testimonies becomes the strong holds in one's life, revises faith, giving purpose to appreciate where you have been and the strive for better living.

Prayer

God is the supreme being, creator and the principle of prayer, he is omnipotent (all powerful), omniscient (all knowing) omnipresent (all present) omnibenevolent (all Good) having all power over eternal existence. Noted in Psalms 47:7 " For God is King of all the earth: sing ye praises with understanding.

Prayer is your free App to direct communication to God for all things, your personal conversation and your loyalty of the order of worship. Noted in Psalms 28:2 "Hereafter the voice of my petitions when I cry to you, when I lift up my hands towards you most holy place"

Kingdom Apostolic Ministries on Sunday morning worship (8-9-20), by Bishop Lambert Gates Jr. Inspiring his listeners saying that " Prayer navigates your life because "prayer changes things". It's time to use our petition for our needs both mentally and physically. Prayers is most efficient during the time of plagues like the Coronavirus and its future variants, where God acknowledges our cries through prayer.

The world has heated up in a wave of destruction because of negative behavioral actions of disobedience. To correct these negative behaviors, we must ask God for grace and mercy for change, we most used the tool that works with God, praying cannot be ignored. You must act on your belief and know God's changing hand works with prayer, prayed by you.

Knowing all the things that make life easier the most thing to acknowledge is God's Grace. The world has come to know the power of **grace,** senior CNN analyst Kirsten Power notes in 2021, she believes people need to activate more towards **grace** from a Biblical point of view to achieve humanity.

The Biblical word **grace** comes from a word that means lovingkindness coming from God. God gives you power through **grace**, to achieve what is needed to accomplish a sense of humanity. God gives you power to avoid bowing down to sinful ways against yourself and mankind. Without God's **grace** you forfeit your opportunity to achieve your highest height. To accomplish grace is noted in Ephesians 2:8 notes "For by **grace** are you saved through faith; and that not of yourself; it is the gift of God" **Grace** is woven in America's fabric, when we say "America the beautiful, this defines us in lyrics "America, America, God shed his **grace** on thee and crown thy good with brotherhood from sea to shining sea!" lyrics America wants honored.

HARMONIZING ROLES

Biblical history has been woven into our existence, therefore we must learn as women and men to take a duel role in building our families with productive personal portfolios to better living. To note the constitution is one document and the Bible is another document, both have similarities to govern natural and spiritual attitudes and behaviors, every effort should be made to harmonize your life as one operation.

Setting the speed dial forward to the present, we must take a good look at the purpose of men, women and child, held in America and across the country. We must take our lives back, become self-managed and in-charge of building one's own lifestyle, starting right now.

The "New Day" in America is centered around technology and Artificial Intelligence, robots have little weaknesses and no heart. Artificial Intelligence objective is to down size the human workforce into a digital computerize economy, it's the new kid on the block.

Creating personal portfolios is necessary to perpetuate growth in family enrichment, building financial foundations, higher learning, character building, increasing spirituality through faith and beliefs which makes you a powerful human being.

Progressive learning includes learning how to live a natural and spiritual life at the same time. The spiritual role has dominancy to provide better earthly living. Gods theology involves dominion over the world noted (Palms 24:1) "The earth is the lord's and fullness thereof: the world and to they that dwell their in." All you need is clarity about Jesus Christ and you will have taken another step towards understanding the importance of your life.

Faith is very important to stimulate the thought process, triggers cognitive thinking which empowers the brain to act to produce good solid behavior, this concept helps the brain to process information for guidance and direction that should give you the energy needed to improve healthy living.

Expectations and accountability for all individuals is held by our society's norms, which have been set in place since ancient times. We live in a society that expects everyone to become self-sufficient, independent and accountable in building healthy life styles. In building one's lifestyle you will need the necessary tools and skills to manage and maintain that life style.

Knowledge is the gateway to understanding the courage needed to put yourself in the right direction and give expression of letting God help you with your dreams, remember if you want to live the dream, you have to work towards your dreams. Nothing is free in America, knowledge is the key to success, without knowledge your life will have limitations when trying to earn your way.

America does offer a piece of the American pie (American Dream) your education will determine how big of a piece of the American dream you will need to succeed. The new approach for change, starts with the informational tower, the brain filled with information to lead you in the world of Artificial Intelligence.

Artificial Intelligence is leading the future, the new kid on the block in taking millions of Jobs replaced by computers. In this arena will require human intelligence, perception, speech recognition, problem solving, decision making and translation of languages to be a part of the new world.

Everyone on this planet will be affected by computered decisions, we have now become global computerized minded. Wealth has become an all-time high for a certain new culture of individuals on their way to millionaire and billionaire status without sharing. This group has become the people's enemy, they are not sharing in the wealth. Will the people in charge keep their spirituality in check over greed that normally reflects self-syndrome known as me, myself and I?

Purpose

Your life is created to have purpose to reflect who you are. Purpose is a movement, continuous working towards a strong development. Knowing your purpose allows you to create new mind sets of good character and a high self-esteem. A new perception arises to have courage's to architect your own life in areas that counts.

Purpose is integrated into your character which identifies your personality to reflect your purpose. Denzel Washington and Phylicia Rashad saw a light of performing art burning in Chadwick Boseman, both extraordinary performing artists took an interest in Boseman. Denzel and Phylicia both devoted time and effort toward helping Chadwick Boseman raise his bar in his acting career.

Rising to the top allowed Actor Boseman remarkable acting and performance abilities to move to the front row of the film Industry. No one else on the earth could of play this role any better than Chadwick Boseman magnificent performance in the portrayal of " James Brown" an old saying" his performance was off the chain" Chadwick Boseman notes, "Purpose is shaped by you" We salute in memory this honorable man Chadwick Boseman.

Education

The greatest tools needed in your life is on-going education, which is the greatest empire in the world. Education holds the key to endless learning connecting knowledge revealing the secrets to becoming a champion to develop a wholesome life style. A strong purpose of character building through education awareness handles patience, endurance, perseverance and persistence under the banner of education.

Educating yourself is the boardwalk to developing your walk into a masterpiece, you must stay ready for all things that may happen in our lives. We must build a personal portfolio that reflects healthy living and stop letting others direct your path, give Jesus that responsibility. In order to deliver better performances in daily living, this comes with daily practice and patience.

Each person should be responsible for designing their own personal portfolio and to create a positive support system. A strong support system helps creates avenues to develop a solid personal portfolio and a personal relationship with God, that has the power to see you through your plans.

It is very important that you learn how to operate and perform in a carnal manner(earthly) and a spiritual manner, two components working in harmony to accomplish healthy living and spiritual gratification, all life is precious. Included in the plan should be short term objectives that will turn into long term goals which helps to build a successful personal portfolio for you and your family.

Self-management has to be another new approach for change, society demands for everyone to be responsible for self, so why not be in-charge. We must act like bulldogs with a bite for change with our spirituality in our hearts. Preparing for the journey through knowledge, plays a major role because knowledge open doors. Your position to move forward depends on how much knowledge you are willing to learn or already have. Productive self-management carries a degree of good decision-making skills to help yourself to build the lifestyle that is best for you.

Life is a never-ending cycle and knowledge is the school of life, only knowledge can open doors. Knowledge entertains its own message, an institution in its self, creating foundations through factual evidence, tested research, investigations and factual studies. Knowledge used correctly host concrete, factual and truthful information, making you champion over your own life. Knowledge keeps us in control and gives us direction to become better builders of healthy living and career makers.

True knowledge is an instrument that helps build solid foundations, removing smoke-screens and dark shadows. Bringing one into the light of things and the real deal about life, today our performance has to be in the category of master work to live. Your life is in your hands, you may not see it for society's dark side, quoting "all for me and none for you" but as long as you have God in your life, worries will be short.

When speaking on knowledge one may wonder how do we keep and maintain this knowledge? God has given us a powerful brain to help us meet the challenges to get the job done. The brain is a powerful weapon, it controls both the physical and mental part of the body. The brain is a store house, one may say the brain is a sponge that can store unlimited amount of information and memory. The brain will empower individuals in preparing their healthy life style.

The brain has full controls for the operations of cognitive thinking and has no time to be dormant, the old saying" The mind is a terrible thing to waste" Cognitive thinking can advance your empowerment of self with the proper training. The mind(brain) controls your knowledge base where cognitive thinking takes place, it's up to each individual to fill his or her brain with the necessary information to be stored for usage at any time to assist in healthy living. Educational achievement comes from seeking a variety of information that can be stored in the brain.

The mind is your fueling power for the battle field where everything takes place in your life. The mind should know and operate on the truth to function properly to maintain continuous growth. This message provides you with a clear understanding on how two minds work together to manage your earthly living and let spirituality lead the way. "Remember the biggest asset we own is our brain, which operates like a sponge, storing unlimited amount of information."

Our lives have been taken from our store houses because of the lack of knowledge, letting computers think for us has been proven to era. Noted (Hosea 5:6) My people are destroyed for lack of knowledge, because thou have rejected knowledge, I will also reject thee, that thou shalt be no priest to me; seeing thou hast forgotten the law of God, I will also forget thy children" These are God's words, where God enforces the knowledge you need to manage your life.

Change takes intensified reconstruction in rebuilding self, you want your natural life to line up with your spiritual life. The toughness of reconstruction comes from damaging conditioning and false mind sets society has imposed with fake news standing in the way of rightful knowledge and Information. Knowledge is also needed to understand, humanity, morality, ethnics, human characteristics, negative and positive energies. Knowledge helps you rise to the occasion of making a difference in your life.

Individual's knowledge-based agenda should include, learning the proper problem-solving skills, such as problem recognition (where the problems lies), identification (causes), gathering information, and the final step, making the decision.

Another important knowledge-based skill on the agenda would be learning more about emotional intelligence. Understanding how your emotions can affect your decision-making skills. Emotions can hijack your rational thinking and get in the way of good decision making. When making decision some time pressures can rule your emotional feelings, causing you not to pay attention to the rational mind in helping you make better decisions. Having emotional intelligence skills builds on good character.

Character building tools helps to fine tune your character in areas of attitudes, integrity, leadership, communication, self-confidence and humility which is an agent for humanity, these skills are certainly an asset to self-management.

Spiritual knowledge gained through biblical scriptures are everything when building your personal portfolios, spirituality protects your design. Spirituality must now be the boss in the room and in charge when planning your personal portfolio.

EXTORTIONARY WOMEN

flowers are most beautiful when they are in full Blossom, the season is here and the timing is now, women blossoming gracefully in bearing good fruit. Extortionary human beings holding their symbols to "Mothers of the earth and caretakers for humanity." Faith is King is proud to salute these wonderful trophies highlighting praises to all female gender young and old.

God has made it known today, he is empowering women more rapidly into leadership domains. Noted in Psalms 46:5 "God is in the mist of her; she shall not be moved, God shall help her, and that right early" Women uncovering their fabrics of humanity, letting the world know, a woman's love also make the world go around.

It is important to note that God has always supported women noted in Luke 1:45 "And blessed is she who believed that there would be a fulfillment of what was spoken to her from God". The message is clear by God for women to surround themselves with spikes of humanity, this is not tug of war with men vs women, God has given gifts to both female and male to exercise their position to help service his earthly people.

Our nation looks through clear lenses, in describing women of all colors, a perceptive view in acknowledging today's women and their involvement in taking leadership roles with guidance and truth. Women leadership comes from integrity of the heart working to do good. Noted in Gelatins 6:9 "Let us not become weary in doing good, for at the proper time we will reap a harvest, if we do not give up." Mothers seem not to ever give up, she is always fighting for the light in her children and her love is brighter than the stars above.

Women becoming more courageous and taking on positions in daily living, whether they get credit or not. The natural spirituality of a women coincide with the messages God makes available in the book of Psalms 27:14 "Wait patiently for the lord, be brave and courageous" an ownership of being a humanitarian.

Strong women movements surfaced around 1848-1917 marching forward for change, because women realize how important their lives are and it's time to take actions to empower themselves. One of the first important battle women faced were fighting for the rights for women to vote in America. The 19th amendment would give women a right to vote.

Women determined to fight for their rights went to the streets to start their campaigns, and were faced with unbearable struggles, agitations, lobbying and civil disobedience. The journey was lengthy and took decades, but these women were determined to reach their goals. Determined women went to the battlefield and victory became their golden kind of day on Aug 18,1920 the right for women to vote was ratified, by the United States congress.

Moving forward with small changes in the 70's, women experienced the era of women liberation thrown back in their faces, where men held women accountable for the thought of being liberated especially in the work force. During this time, if a woman couldn't lift the requirement of a man, she could be fired, companies ran by men, did not want to adjust weigh capacity for women they admired at home, in the kitchen or the bedroom, but no acceleration for women in the work force.

Women began to realize how important their lives were and they started to act to empower themselves. Today women have empowered themselves to stand behind no one, when making contributions in turning the wheels for society.

Women have always established themselves with a build in radar system to guide themselves in life. Even in the Bible, Adam mentions that Eve was the "Mother of life." A woman produces the DNA for every human existence, used to identify human beings. No person's DNA is the same it's one of a kind for each and every one of us, created by a woman.

A woman carries a natural insight to lead, processing her creative mind to work her body and soul to her maximum, to conquer the unknown when there's little light at the end of the tunnel. She embraces the impossible for herself and her family and when men sometimes feels defeated, she comes out the corner boxing, looking for a victory with her rugged charm. She is a great human being, she creates miracles in the reproduction of life.

Today the chains have been broken, women and their opportunity are an open door to the battle grounds. James Brown said it best "This is a man's world, but it would be nothing without a woman or a girl" (Published by James Brown in July 11, 2017) James Brown explaining" the world would be nothing without a **Woman** or a **Girl**" right on James Brown".

God have shown us many examples of women humanitarians demonstrated through God's choice, like **Ruth** in the Bible, who had a declaration and a commitment to Naomi her mother in-law who loved the Lord. Ruth knew Naomi was old and needed attention in maintaining life, so Ruth stayed by her side. By Ruth living under God's way her journey of emptiness became fulfilment and blessed simply because she demonstrated humanity.

Queen Sheba a powerful female monarch ruler of Ethiopia believed in Paganism Gods, she had heard of the great King Solomon being the wisest King in the world and was curious about his empire. (I Kings 10:1) When the Queen of Sheba heard of the fame of Solomon concerning the name of the Lord, she came to him with questions. He was also known for his wisdom, fame and his loyalty to Judaism. Queen Sheba traveled to see him, to test his wisdom and to view his great monuments he had built for the Lord.

Queen Sheba brought to King Solomon a train of camels, spices, gold, and precious stone. Queen Sheba set with King Solomon to sharpen her skills using his advice and counseling to build Ethiopia into a better empire. (I King 10:6 "And she said to the King, it was a true report that I heard in mine own land of the acts and of thy wisdom"

King Solomon was admired by Queen Sheba and showed his humanity noted (I kings 10:13)"And King Solomon gave unto the Queen of Sheba all her desire whatsoever she asked" After the prominent visit with King Solomon she returned to Ethiopia, God gave her grace and the power of judgement because she seen with her own eyes the knowledge of God's Holy theology and reign with a Solomonic power that had an end effect on both Egypt and Ethiopia, she had positioned herself with God to reign with humanity all over the country she ruled.

It's amazing how God creates natural things like the northern star as a guide in helping people to freedom. This woman born 1822 in Dorchester county, Maryland, her name is Tice David, better known **as Harriett Tubman**, A courageous adversary willing to put her life on the line for justice, moving African American slaves from the south to the north to freedom.

Harriett Tubman made 19 trips, freeing 300 slaves with a bounty on her head of $40,000. The bounty was not as important as the freedom for human lives that suffered from unbearable treatment, bad living condition, physical and mental harassment, even experiencing a horrible death as hanging.

She was a fearless warrior in the wilderness of the unknown traveling with God grace and guidance, listening carefully to the voice of God for the right direction to freedom. They called her "Black Moses" because her mission was the same type of mission as Moses in the bible, instructed by God for Moses to go get his people out of bondage in Egypt. Sister Tubman did not stop demonstrating her humanity with the underground railroad, but involved herself as a nurse, launchers, and a union spy against slavery. She was a woman with deep Christian faith, planted in her heart to achieve true humanity.

Hattie McDaniel's was an extortionary actress, born June 10,1893, her talented acting flourished in "Gone with The Wind," a high profiled movie that projected slavery and the fine living of white southern Americans. Hattie McDaniel became a star born to stardom. In the mist of thick racism, she became the first African American woman to win an Oscar. Hattie McDaniel famous quotes" I did my best and God did the rest" a magnificent trail brazier, made a huge contribution to African American experience.

Eleanor Roosevelt was a pioneer for humanity during a tough era for America, she was a trail brazier for women's movement, worked with the Red Cross during War I. Eleanor joined the league of women voters, worked with child care welfare, housing reform, equal rights for women and racial minorities.

Eleanor Roosevelt demonstrated her position for human rights, standing for all, but especially for an African American opera singer Marian Anderson, who were forbidden by the Daughters of the American Revolution (DAR) to sing at Constitutional Hall, Eleanor Roosevelt resigned from the Daughters of American Revolution organization and used her authority to have the event at the Lincoln Memorial where 75,000 attended.

Eleanor Roosevelt involved herself with the first Black Tuskegee Airman, where she took an airplane ride with a Tuskegee airman to support their efforts. Eleanor Roosevelt was just a rebel for humanity, God knew just where to place her acts of humanity, during the crucial fight for civil rights for all.

This great woman's voice still rings in America's atmosphere, saying " You must try to do the things you think you cannot do "Eleanor Roosevelt greatness covers far more than a writer could write explaining her humanity. When we are born only God knows our direction, in what he wants individuals to represent and accomplish.

Leadership positions takes courage to be active in America's political world of politics, during the 70's, especially when the door seemed shut even under the constitution representing African Americans Shirley **Chisholm, Born** Nov 30, 1924 was the first American woman to be elected to the United States of congress, representing 12 congressional districts in New York.

Shirley Chisholm's leadership abilities were highly favored, the first African American woman in 192 years to handle congressional grassroots affairs in the democratic national party's business. An extraordinary presidential woman equipped with leadership skills in early childhood welfare, education, educational consultant, activist for the labor committee and founding member of the Woman's National Political Committee.

In 1972 Shirley Chisholm ran for a democratic nomination for the President of the United States. Shirley Chisholm is a national figure and shines a bright light in being a cornerstone for women who also takes self-worth as a constitution to the need of America.

Shirley Chisholm were fearless when it came to the welfare of the people, her leadership of integrity came from the heart' noted in Isaiah 41:10 "So do not fear; I am with you do not be dismayed, for I am your God, I will strengthen you and help you; I will uphold you with my righteous hand" Those words are the fuel Shirley Chisholm used to climb towards the mountain top.

Born January 29, 1954 in Kosciusko, Mississippi and grew up in dire poverty, she was raised by her grandmother Hallie Mae Lee who was active in her life. Her name is **Oprah Winfrey**, God gave her a gift to service using her abilities and skills needed in the role of humanity.

Oprah Windfrey came up in the 1950's, racism extending its way through her career. Oprah waking up to worldwide racism, expositions, systems grabbing at her success. Gold diggers spent little to no energy to help Ms. Windfrey succeed, only to finds ways to take her revenue by accusing her of having a bad beef conversation, claiming the conversation caused an effect on the sale of the beef industry in Texas. The beef industry already dealing with the mad cow revelation, way before any conversations by Oprah Windfrey, but still the cattle industry tried to put the blame on MS Windfrey but failed. You mean to tell me this little black woman had that much power, to stop the Texans and the rest of the world from eating beef, "Oh give me a break America!"

During Oprah's Era, women's hardship was experiencing a

struggle for equality and respect as a woman in the world of success. She was the youngest African American to anchor the news in Nashville WTVF-TV. Her strive demonstrated many extraordinary accomplishments and contributions. In 2008 she created her own Oprah Winfrey network and lead the way in programming, connecting social media and global culture.

Oprah Windfrey stepping into the movies sector was even a greater success, in her performance in the movie "Beloved" represented by Touchstone pictures based on a Pulitzer Prize winning novel by Toni Morrison, Christmas Dog 2007 co- produced by Harpo films and the Weinstein Co, releases the movie the Great Debater starring Denzel Washington. One of our great favorites and talented movies the "**Color Purple**" by Steven Spielberg where Orpah received an Academy Award and Golden Globe nominations. The Color Purple gave the audience a capture of southern black families, who made their lives meaningful.

She is a solidary woman and a quiet storm of many awards in 2013, where she was honored with the Presidential Medal of Freedom. Oprah Windfrey is the treasure of humanity, she has extended her services in many areas of creating hundreds of grants to support empowering organizations in support of education, empowerment for women's, children and family care.

Ms. Windfrey lifts her heart and spirit to the motherland of children in South Africa, she calls the mission Christmas Kindness in South Africa. She has represented her kindness with her own revenue for better and healthy living all of the world. Ms. Oprah Windfrey creates good fruit. What every she touches turns gold, which God turns her efforts into success. Oprah Windfrey lights shines when she reaches out for the shining lights in others. Ms. Oprah Winfrey has a golden stamp of approval in the eyes of humanity.

Our talents are given by God, he uses talents to lift our spirits of joy in song and celebrations, A dedicated Diva to her profession born March 25, 1942 in Memphis Tennessee and resided in Detroit, Michigan. Her Name is **Aethra Franklin,** she started her singing career at 14, traveling with her father C.L. Franklin's revivals. Aethra experience an early grown-up life, she became a mother at a young age, but no matter the struggle she triumphed her way to fame.

Aethra Franklin were part of the Motown sound and lacey in Detroit, Michigan, Motown's birth place, where Motown streaming takes place with an International destiny and a pilgrimage for the musical stars of the future.

When God give you a gift to shine, your dedication will flow (Palms 89:1) " I will sing of the mercies of the lord forever, with my mouth will I make known thy faithfulness to all generations" Aethra Franklin voice is like a humming bird, singing all over the world, singing to the get down of rock to the comfort of jazzy melodies, while taking the gospels right to the soul. Alethea Franklin's talents sky rockets to the highest notes in Opera for the stars in heaven to twinkle, as Mayo Angelo says just a "Phenomenal woman".

Aretha was a musical genius, a champion of song, she was a song writer, actress, and a pianist. In 1972 her album Amazing Grace was nominated for an NME award and sold over two million copies in 1987. Aretha Franklin became the first female artist to be inducted into the Rock and Roll Hall of Fame, in 2008 won 18 gram my awards. Aretha Franklin loved by many was honored, when asked to sing the National Anthem to begin the 2009 democratic national convention, at President Barack Obama Inauguration. In her career she sold 75million records nationwide because her voice became a natural resource singing around the world.

In her collection of humanity Aretha Franklin travels were many, she walked with Martin Luther King on the "**Freedom Walk**", where he spoke to 100,000 people **" I have a Dream "** In her era she dedicated herself, singing all over the country raising money for civil rights organizations, she even extended her charity, when spelling out humanity in bailing Angle Davis out of jail in Detroit during the civil rights movement. Her financial giving to humanity reaches many, coming straight from her heart. Aretha Franklin was always appreciated at thanksgiving in Detroit with her performance and a grand turkey dinner for all that came.

Aretha Franklin never lost focus on God gift to her, she quotes "

My **faith** always have been and always will be important " Her faith in God was always by her side, she was a "natural woman" asking the world for a **"Little "Respect"**, she is the **"Queen of Soul"**.

God assigns individuals also who are in high places to accomplish his work, a stunning intellectual beauty inside and out, her radiant smiles brings a glow in people's heart when she reaches so many. Her smiles tell us that she is pleased with herself in the things she has achieved. Her name is **Michelle Robinson Obama.** Born January 17,1964 to Mr. and Mrs. Fraser Robinson on the southside of Chicago, Illinois. Michelle was an educational scholar from the get go, she graduated at Whitney Young high school. Knowing that she would continue to invest in her education, in 1985 received a Bachelor of Arts at Princeton University, reaching for higher education, she attended law school at Harvard University.

The strive for accomplishments and experienced came knocking at her door, she became a Junior associate working with Chicago Mayor Richard M. Daly and worked also with the Chicago's Department of Planning and Development. As time moved forward God bless her with a perfect union where she married Barack Obama and later had two daughters.

Two unstoppable forces for humanity has join together taking on the national nominee for President of the United States of America. Michelle Obama work diligently beside her husband candidacy, strategically working with her husband on plans to become president. The victory came, Barack Obama became 44th president of the United States of America and she became the first African American first lady of the president of the United States.

Extraordinary remarkable Lawyers, working side by side, speeding up the cure for humanity, but when it came time to stand alone, Michelle Obama demonstrates her leadership many times in different places, became an author spreading humanity in a language that everyone understood. Michelle Obama also worked brilliantly helping military families and early childhood obesity.

In 2015 Michelle worked with President Barack Obama in launching a global program, helping young women with life skill preparations to become independent. Michelle stood strong in supporting rightful organizations as "Black Girls Rock" such a phenomenal woman. Words to remember from Michelle Obama, this great lady "Be comfortable with a little greatness"

God maintains his people in authority, to ensure that the fight for truth stands, choosing advocates, who has generational history of being a humanitarian through their career efforts is a strong factor in caring the torch for humanity. Raised in a political family, she maintains her aspiration in the spirit of Democracy. Her Name is **Nancey Pelosi** born 1940 in Baltimore Maryland, raised up in a Roman Catholic family and a strong democratic neighborhood. Nancy graduated from Trinity College in Washington D.C. where she received a Bachelor Degree in political science.

Nancy Pelosi started her political strive at 12 years old, attending her first democratic convention. Pressing her way through the ranks of politic, her strength began to surface. Nancy was a front runner when it came to effective fundraising, the first woman to lead a party in congress and also became White house minority leader.

The hard work of a political strategist took her to becoming speaker of the house in 2019. In congress there are two positions to be represented, self-interest or for the people. A general Nancy Pelosi in the House of Representative is strictly working for the people, by the oath she took no matter the battle, she is always in the front row for Democracy (Psalms 119:106) "I have sworn and I will perform it, that I will keep thy righteous judgement" and Nancy has been approved by her dedication of performance to her highest ability.

Nancy Pelosi took a step further in the visit of Taiwan on Aug 3, 2022 a pledge she kept with the Twainian people in support to continue a democratic system. China had threatened her visit to Taiwan, but her loyalty stood fast and her visit had been pledged, regardless of the roaring lion Xi Jinping retaliation promised. Nancy Pelosi was in the hands of God, noted in 1 Samuel 22: 3 " The God of my rock; in him will I trust; he is my shield, and the horn of my salvation, my savior; thou savest me from violence "as prayers went out as she traveled from China and back safely to America, those prayers to God gave Nancy Pelosi the promise.

Nancy Pelosi integrity calls for "Unity" at all cost, enhances her leadership skills to get the job done, her courage speaks out for social justice and reform and the roar in her voice means business at hand. The vision for healthy living for Americans has always been her focus and she has never been afraid to let prayer lead the way.

Nancey Pelosi is stepping down from her position as speaker of the house, passing the Paton to qualified youthfulness leaders of tomorrow, in leading the paths of democracy in an ever-changing world. History will never forget Nancy Pelosi, an elite global warrior for Democracy, God bless all her future endeavors.

An Ice breaker in performing arts, took her audience around the world and back, born Nov 13, 1955. **Caryn Elaine Johnson,** but her audience, fans and lovers of art, know her as **Whoopi Goldberg,** a New Yorker. Whoopi Goldberg traveled the distant of unknown territories as an African American front runner for television, theater and movie screens performances. Holding graciously countless awards such as the **EGOT, which includes an Emmy Award, Grammy Award, Academy Award, and a Tony Award,** all reflecting her greatness.

Whoopi Goldberg formulated comedy that only she could achieve and her gifts of talents reached unbelievable heights. As she traveled the distant of her remarkable acting, an **Oscar** had crown her as best supporting actress in 1991 in the movie "Ghost."

Whoopi Goldberg talents has many turns until even her voice has become gold, illustrated in the Lion King and Toy story 3. Let's not forget one of the world's favorite the **"Color Purple"** where her performance was sensational. Whoopi Goldberg has so many well achieved performances until we must close with her current energy the "View" where she embraces and articulate liberal views, Whoopi Goldberg, such a phenomenal woman!

Young strong commander in her performance and a true Michigander born August 23,1971, raised in Grand Rapids, her name is **Gretchen Esther, Whitmer.** Taking on responsibility at

14, took her first job working for Burlingame Lumbers Co. Reaching for higher education, attended Michigan State University receiving a B.A in Education. Striving for higher education became a graduate of Michigan State Law School. Moving forward in her life she became a loving wife and a wonderful mother.

Gretchen Whitmer record stands for itself, she was a former legislator, prosecutor and served from 2001 -2006 in the Michigan House of Representatives. Gov Whitmer holds onto grass root ideologies, listening to others to create change, a problem solver and negotiator. She has humanity deep down in her soul to command justice for domestic violence and sexual assault, rehabilitation of non-violent first-time offenders, working to improve better education and up to date skill training across the board. Gov. Gretchen Whitmer leads the way in Michigan repairing and restoring Michigan's infrastructure.

In 2020 Gov Gretchen Whitmer faced the biggest and worst crisis in her career the Coravirus Pandemic that covered the world. When odds seem to be against her, she stood like a rock that could not be move and used her expertise, experience, resources, knowledge, and strong strategically planning to pulled Michigan out of the hot spots and reduce the peak of the Coronavirus to protect the vulnerable and save lives.

We salute this commander and chief, the governor of Michigan, a General on the battlefield. President Trump targeted a violent ransom to down size Gov. Whitmer, by supporting militia activity to take her life. With the virus in one hand and death threats in the other hand, fear did not stop her from being a true governor and protecting the State of Michigan.

Spirituality supports Gov Whitmer attitude and faith in administrating in the right direction noted in Isiah 41:10 "So do not fear, for I am with you do not be dismayed, for I am your God, I will strengthen you and help you; I will uphold you with my righteous right hand" and God did what he promised, he protected her, when others tried to take her life. In 2022 Gov. Whitmer won her crown to stay on the battlefield with greatness and hard work for Michigan. God bless her in all her administrating endeavors.

Ruth Bada Ginsburg born March 15, 1933 in Brooklyn New York, Ruth came from a struggling family, confident in overcoming the obstacles of life. Ruth Ginsburg the second female justice of the U.S. Supreme Court, spent her lifetime representing the fight for the rights of women, gender discrimination, and advocating true justice for all

Ruth Ginsburg was respected from her colleagues on both side of the democratic Ilse and the community, an advocate for justice. Blazing the same humanitarian trail for justice as Thurgood Marshall an associate supreme court justice of the United States, known for his fight in Brown vs Board of Education. advocating equal rights for African American children to have equal education.

Women have continuously faced the facts in fighting against male controlling figures, women demanding their voices to be heard for equal rights. Equal in everything's that matter in building a bigger and better America. Ruth Ginsburg knew and lived the challenge by saying "I ask no favor for my sex, all I ask of our brethren is that they take their feet off our necks"

Ruth Ginsburg is also honored for her inspiring model to be herself, identifying with Christopher Wallace, a legendary rapper nickname "Notorious Big" and in past conversations, Ruth Ginsburg represents herself also known as "Notorious" Ruth Ginsburg proud in sharing the name "Notorious "with Christopher Wallace, there was no shame in her game. In memory of the great supreme court Justice Ruth Ginsburg.

Keisha Lance Bottom born January 18,1970 in Atlanta Georgia, making her mark as an American politician and highly rated lawyer. Experienced to govern her beloved city Atlanta Georgia, held positions in 3 different branches of government. Mayor Bottom partner's herself with progressive efforts in equity, diversity and inclusion, advocate against human tariffing and working continuously for better policies and conditions towards individual experiencing state corrections.

Governor Brian Kemp (Republican) of Georgia tried to silence Mayor Keisha Lane Bottom with his aggressive actions, in trying to maintain power, control and rule in representing the Republican Reds, his republican membership also wanted to turn Democracy into republican control. The threat was not big enough to stop Mayor Keisha Lance Bottoms, doing what leaders do, provide and protect healthy living for Georgians.

Mayor Bottom soldiered up when the Coronavirus hit the state of Atlanta Georgia, giving professional guidance through the help of science, professionals and community involvement, making Atlanteans health the prime focal point for recovery against the killer virus.

Mayor Bottom and her family became a victim of the infecting killer virus, but the virus did not stop the wounded warrior. Under health illness she never left the battlefield, knowing what was ahead she took on John Lewis philosophy "Good Trouble" was worth her dedication. Former Mayor Bottom now standing in the ranks of President Biden, appointed to the office of public engagement to focus on families for healthier living.

There are so many different contributions women have made until books could not hold the writing. A short narrative of women in professional sports arenas must be honored. Tennis historians will always remember the champions in the game of tennis. This highlight shines on two sisters who have open doors and left their tennis statement all over the world. Two-great legacies in the game of professional tennis and others in the game as well.

Professional highlights began with **Serena Williams and Venus Williams** Two African American tennis "super stars" both reaching the heights of being number 1 and champions on and off the courts. Whether they played together or against each other they never lost their grace for **sisterhood.**

Serena a grand slam champion, hitting balls to her opponents at the speed of 128 mph making her mark known. Venus off the court in the mist of her travels, in 2007 Venus efforts was accomplished, breaking the barrier of being the first women to earn exactly the same as Roger Renderer.

Serena and Venus Williams are the trail blazers who can now reach back, grab a hand in role modeling for upcoming courageous young women trying to make their mark also in the game of professional tennis. Inspired by Serena Williams, **Coco Gaff** the youngest African Atlanta peach, ranked in the top 100 by the Women's Tennis Association. **Naomi Osaka's** of Japan, winner of the 2020 U.S. open. A prominent athlete, masking up to stand for Black Lives Matter showing courage to stand for America's reality. We salute and crown these professional trail blazers for the future ahead.

Faith is King salutes all women all over the world, shining a light on their beauty, intellect, and contributions. Always remember God gave us these activists to represent and maintain humanity.

Kamala Harris Born Oct 20, 1964 has become a great American politician, inherited a generational gift in public service from her parents, Shyamalan Gopalan her mother a scientist and researcher, her father Donald Harris, a professor in economics. Kamala Harris childhood atmosphere was centered around both talented parents being strong participating advocates for human civil rights. Most of all her mother always maintained her Indian Tamil Afro Jamaican cultural enrichment with her children.

Senator Kamala Harris has an extortionary background, attended Howard University and Hastings College of Law. Kamala Harris was the former Attorney General of California, district attorney for San Francisco and now the first African American women to become Vice President of the United States of America.

Vice president Harris has the passion to be responsible for the oaths she's taken in public service, always acts as a facilitator for problem solving her duties, communicating that voices will be heard, her leadership grounded in courage to make the rightful decisions for the American people. Her voice rings out to the nation lets rebuild our nation together. Vice president Harris position has great responsibility to be the tie breaker in solving problems in our congress today.

Most of all vice president Kamala Harris in her conversation gives praises to her mother for the seeds set in her life, she knows mothers are the greatest in the world, mothers are our heart beats in our lives and the lights in our eyes. When we fall, our mothers pick us up and her motherly smile brings sunshine when our days seem blue.

When we talk about future greatness, we commend and celebrate our young adults, who takes the spotlight. Her Name is **Amanda S.C. Gorman** an award-winning writer and a Harvard graduate "Com Lauda." Amanda Gorman extending her humanity in poetry, publishing "The one for whom food is not enough"

Amanda Gorman's travels for humanity is just her beginning, she is engaged as an activist fighting to stamp out oppression, feminism, race and marginalization, as well as the African diaspora. Amanda the youngest Inauguration poet, was chosen by first lady Jill Biden to address the nation on January 20, 2021, her topic "The hill we climb."

Amanda's radiant black beauty shining across the capitol atmosphere expresses in spoken words, the condition of America's soul and the need for healing, "Democracy can be delayed, never defeated" as she continues to shine saying "Only if we are brave enough to see it------------- Her spoken words penetrated her audience soul, calling for the nation's healing, recognizing that only truth can fix it.

Amanda Gorman was asked a huge question, who inspired her and she said "My Mother", Joan Wicks a Northwestern University graduate, not an ordinary mother, but a mother who created pathways for her children and an example for her family. Nina Simone lyrics could not describe Amanda Gorman any better as a representation of her musical theory "She is young, gifted and Black" **Ms. Nina Simone** a national trail brazier for human rights demonstrates power in songs, stepping over life with courage to sing the songs of sin and pain society played upon Black culture's soul, never to win the American dream. The souls of African Americans have been sold in song, she expresses how discrimination has been woven in America. Still the great Nina Simone just wanted the acceptance of America in song, singing it's a new dawn, a new day, a new life just for me and I'm feeling good **"Freedom is mine"**

One of the Greatest Icon every live was Ms. Cicely Tyson Born Dec. 18, 1921 in Harlem New York to **two spiritual** parents, Cicely Tyson sieged the screen with elegancy and dignity as an American actress that commanded that her characters in acting be meaningful. She shines a light on scripts that elevated her cause to navigated the beauty of a Black American actress. She was a prime example for others following the same trail in the world of acting.

In 2016 Cicely Tyson received the "Medal of Freedom" given by President Obama. Playing roles across the spectrum in the art of acting, was a prize in the eyes of the world with roles in Sounder, Autobiography of Miss Jane Pitman, Roots and many more. Cicely Tyson acting became a movement share with many, her gold stamp has been approved all over the spectrum of acting in memory of the Great! Great! Icon of acting who went home to glory on January 29,2021

There is a celebration message for all women who are making a difference in the lives of others. Great women with creative ideas are hummy birds for the future. No acknowledgement is necessary when you have faith in yourself to succeed, because your crown never leaves you and your light is always shinning even when you may not be mentioned.

NATION'S LIGHTHOUSE

CNN

acknowledgement at its best to CNN extraordinary journalists no matter the titled held. A group of journalists standing for integrity, leading with their hearts to bring currents events, that matters to the American people. News in true fashion to everyone around the world, a team leading us to the truth that effects our daily living regardless of what the political arena addresses about the truth of our realities.

CNN demonstrates quality networking in gathering and sharing news with other networking journalists such as, senior alumni Congressional Correspondent Rachel Scott of ABC news, circling around platforms such as Good Moring America, World news tonight, comes into the circle for the current events in our lives to assist in bringing truth to our ears.

CNN's expertise shares reporting with a multitude of professionals and community advocates seeking the facts. Voicing with messages of reality checks and fact checking to weed out opinion vs facts to stop fake news that has poisoned our society. CNN took the role in America's crisis to be the light house designed to emit light to our eyes and sounds to our ears to face our realities here in America and all over the world.

CNN journalists have demonstrated many times the courage to

open a threat that sits in Panadura's box, letting out the reality where it stands. Turning over every stone where news is hidden, bringing out complicated news to the light for better understanding. CNN gladiators on the ground trudging through unknown territory where reality lies, a badge of bravery bringing the nation the truth.

CNN sets the tone in current events, revealing truth to the American people in important issues that effects lives aboard and around the world. Took a strong stand in important issues such as the "Black Lives Matter" centered around the George Floyd execution by policemen,

CNN news an activist during the Covid 19 crisis and the 2020 presidential election, plowing through information to bring the facts of reality, stamping out any fake news that will tip the scales of destroying humanity.

Journalists asking uncomfortable questions in important matters and exposing violations against the American people. CNN news is the eye opener and in layman's term, operator of news for the American people and around the world. CNN is America's safety net to factual knowledge, bringing truth to national news to hold us together in critical moment of a fatherless country since 2016.

CNN Journalist's news comes from the ground up, fighting their way, sometimes even jailed but still stood strong enough to bring rightful national world news. A village of talented personalities who makes news stay alive. There are no small roles in CNN news rooms and their enterprise, just heroism in delivering historical and current events as it happens even in perilous times.

During the pandemic's early stages, CNN brought news into our living rooms, giant waves of the unexpected, during the crucial critical times of the Pandemic, telling viewers crushing news of the Pandemic's destruction like the mighty waves of the sea and no medical science to fix it.

CNN was like the elements of the earth, letting us know the storms ahead in our lives and the sunshine of truth in our realities. CNN were America's watch tower during Trump's autocracy period, the plan to kill Democracy. CNN was America's light house at the end of the tunnel, seeking a brighter day ahead.

America faced a surrendered President Donald Trump, refusing to help guide through the horrifying stages of the Pandemic, with factional information, a course needed for the American people to depend on. CNN brought in Dr Sanjay Gupta, setting the tone in treating the world as a patient to overcome the killer virus and bring support to the medical front line workers. Dr. Sanjay Gupta created a bridge of comfort to family's listeners who had to be absent from their families, during the worse time of the Pandemic, faced with a non-abiding America.

CNN journalists were in the front row to make a difference in delivering the news during the 2020 presidential election. CNN stood the test of time, letting their expertise guide American people to the truth in the election vote. Journalist stayed focus to the letter, during the election period televising every moment of the count of each state in America.

CNN watchmen kept fraud makers from entering the methods of televised voting it just didn't happen on CNN's watch. Even when the cry baby cried, the election was stolen, CNN stood their ground and brought the news all the way to victory of a new President Biden and Vice President Harris. Democracy thanks founder Ted Turner and CEO Jeff Zucker and the entire staff for their stand on the rights trails of humanity.

SUMMARY

The summary message maybe extensive because it's all about wellness so desperately needed in surrounding the American people. America's history and present–day living experience covers a lot of territory. America's constitutional documents does not cover all the things needed to have a successful life, you must include spiritual guidance to produce successful living. The **message** should be clear, but just to make sure, again the messages written gives clear **factual knowledge** to **understanding** God's **purpose and his promise** for his people in the world he created.

The Bible says that God is the beginning, end and the path to eternal life. God made men and women in his own image (meaning the character of God, not his physical image) gave power to rule over everything noted in (Genesis 2:26). This empowerment was given to the American people to be used for creating a righteous life on earthly ground for the purpose of his creations. The job of men and women today is to be fruitful, multiply and replenish the earth in a righteous way through healthy living.

Historical observation demonstrates all over the world that God blessed American from the beginning of its birth, allowing pioneers to set Americans seeds for Christianity. American pioneers carried God and the Good Book in their hearts to guide them in an unknown land. Building America on symbolic grounds, trusting their lives in the hands of God.

The strength of worship built the melting pot of different types of cultures hosting a power greater than themselves. Americans believing strong enough to parade **"In God we trust"** found on America's currency. Saluting the America flag with "God Bless America and one nation under God."

The True goal of the reading is to invite you to real truth and why we must include the very institution that gives life its balance here in America. The evidence has been clearly layout before us, but we still seem to seek other entities that may not have any value but dreams. It's time to realize that God has an effect on our lives and to stop using God for convenience or in the sign of trouble only.

The full scope of messaging is to be a messenger revealing the truth that our lives has always been built around Jesus Christ's holiness since the beginning of time, yet still today's men and women continue to behave and performed as their historian brother and sisters who also turned away from God. New messaging is to create important conversations that will harmonize Americans towards healthier living with a spiritual attitude holding down a unified front.

The writing is on the wall, America is tipping the scales towards a culture of Babylonian symbolism. Babylon was a great empire back in the time of 29 B.C Messalina Region, Babylon known as the" Doors of the Gods," a weaponized society, where their theology eventually spread into Israel.

The Babylonians developed great inventions towards math, science, writing and many more. Babylon became one of the richest cities every built-in ancient time. Babylon strength hosted top military war agents and the greatest territorial empire every built under the Babylon command. Each conqueror over Babylon had the minds of idolatry, a symbol of man's showmanship of power.

Babylon's destructive behavior was a great sin against God, the culture became so corrupt and unsavory until God's anger caused the Babylonians great destruction. Babylon's great sins against God caused him to react noted in Jeremiah 51:62 "Then shalt thou say, O Lord hast spoken against this place, to cut off, that none shall remain in it, neither man or beast, but that it shall be desolated forever." In

Sept of 1977 dictator Sadden Hussein of Iraq tried to rebuild Babylon but fail, God has kept his **promise.**

In America's Babylonian ideology has filtrated its way into America's society today, greed has become an economical God. Authorities we trusted, steadily empowering themselves in making bad decisions that impacted others' lives as the O'Jays sings "**For the Love of Money"** the Bible sends a bigger message noted in Timothy 6:10 "For the love of money is the **"Root of Evil".** Men and women have become too extreme for the love of themselves and worship of money.

What roads are you traveling that has no signs to direct your path? If you are lost who will you trust for direction to get back on course? Today will men and women turn from their wicked ways to save humanity? America now facing a new sheriff in town that changes the world's attitude, called Artificial Intelligence, has its own throne inside of mankind. A revolutionary technology of change, computers, satellites and robots will be in command of all societies and deliver wealth to the individuals in charge.

American greediness has taken control of our sight to leave us blind to manage our lives. High social media techs, such as Tik-Tok, Instagram and Face book have kept men and women distorted to manage their lives by providing wrongful information, yet deep in our pockets selling our personal information without permission, life now controlled by someone else.

The high-tech industry is exposing our children to unsavory acts without understanding, a 6th grader in Virginia having a dispute with the teacher and brings a gun to school and shoots the teacher. These high-tech exposures leaving children to mock grown- up negative behaviors and actions, but who cares.

Americans holding on to the second amendment with no change, while our children are expose to death time and time again. Still more trouble in the camp with Elon Musk and Twitter, the new owner bringing disorder, confusion and chaos, allowing more reckless hot mic conversations and hate under the freedom of speech on social media, while young future watch grown-up negative behaviors.

This praised Artificial Intelligence can be our worse enemy finding ways to hack into America's security systems, holding America ransom and invading American's land. This is just the beginning of America's roller coaster ride.

America's Intelligence unit in 2021 found cycler attacks on private commercial sectors such as the Colonial Pipe line, who had to ransom themselves back in operation caused by cyber criminals. This current siege caused Americans to experience a panic for gasoline storage and the rise in prices in the eastern states and around the country. JBS Foods were also attacked by cyber attackers who also uses Cryptocurrency, which is hard to track cyber criminals. The biggest cyber-attack in 2022 were SolarWinds supply chain, also noted, 53.35 million Americans citizens experienced personal cyber-attack, including investment fraud in 2022.

Events of cyber-attacks fueled by Russia criminals, constantly hacking in America's E-mail system targeting the US government's pentagon and natural treasury. America is now at extreme risk, already experiencing 15,000 cases or more of cyber-attacks against services needed to survive, such as hospitals, trains, fuel, food and water.

The greediness of man's power today is causing another person's destruction which effects everyone. Economic growth greed has never been intended to be shared and reach the front lines of America's people. Americans has lost faith, while turning the economic wheels for their own society. The picture becomes clearer, the wealthy has no intention to include anyone else but themselves and friends in economic gain.

Noted in Timothy 6:10 "For the love of money is the root of evil". Men and women have become too extreme for the love of themselves and worship of money. Losing sight of humanity caused the wealthy to start implementing weapons of neglect and abuse of human beings. Noted in ll Timothy 6:9" But thy that will be rich fall into temptation and a snare and in to many foolish and hurtful lust, which drown men in destruction and perdition." The greed of man is accelerating God's prophecy of the great coming of God.

The Greed to steal wealth came straight from the top of our government, where Trump and the Republican Reds used the American revenue to increase their empire by using smoke screens, schemes, false conspiracy theories, back door under the table deals and lies to carry the plan out. Who says the Devil does not have power?

The government being led by Trump and the Republican Reds, demonstrated reckless behavior, causing Americans to experience a crisis in a form of a great volcano on American's soil. The eruption spreads as an invisible virus infecting and killing the nation's people, as the hot lava filtrates its way into a mist of many calamities.

America's Administration ruled by Trump lost control of the virus that swept the shores of America. The President defying the directions of the pleading scientist and ignored the signs to hide the Pandemic existence. The refusal to listen caused a life of darkness and death, demonic spirits working through Donald Trump had severe effects on the American people, causing God to bound all actions from Donald Trump and denounced his throne "enough is enough!"

Americans now fighting alone an enemy on their own soil a killer virus, an unknown battle seeking refuge to return home to America's norm. America must face reality about the killer virus to win the war. Alongside the killer virus battle comes the eruption of America's volcano, not calming down, but spilling into an eruption globally with the protest of Black Lives Matter joined with freedom fighters for justice took to the streets against discrimination and racism, rallying against any statue that represents injustice of the people.

Police brutality on the rise with the brutal murder of George Floyd, opening doors of fire to address the expelling of Black Lives Matters calling to stop hate and brutality of black and brown people, who have been victims of racism since blacks hit the shores of Point Comfort in the James Town colony in Virginia under the rule of slavery. History was made finally when other races joined hand to hand in marching for Afro Americans cause, marching to the steps "Enough is Enough"

America must fight together as they travel down the avenues

of redemption in repairing the nation from major players like economical strife, systemic racism, health care and a nation divided at wartime and the true reality, **only "unity"** can fix it.

It is also important to recognize during America's dark moments, the support for America is growing thin, America now fighting with other countries to maintain its power that has been prophesized noted in Matthews 24.7" For the nations shall rise against nations and kingdoms against kingdoms, and there shall be famines, pestilences and earthquakes, in divers' places" These actions will certainly put people into sorrow and suffering experiences.

A prime example today of bible prophecy happened in 2022, when Russia invaded Ukraine, the brutal violent act against God's people in Ukraine has turned the world upside down, causing fear in Europe (a member of NATO) to deploy 300,000 troops to be on alert against Russia.

America's decisions are to defend NATO against a powerful nation like Russia at all cost. Rocky Mountains between countries are erupting everywhere including China, The Anti-Christ is forming noted in the scriptures, before God comes there will be only one-man government that will rule the world, this has been prophesized.

Until God makes his decision to end the madness, continuous natural revelations will be performed my God as a warning of the disobedience of men and women and their lost for love for his people. Warning may cause death but even still, men and women's heart will remain harden and according to thy scriptures **"Wax Cold**. A prime example of **"Wax Cold" is** when president Donald Trump turned his back for 187 minutes and became TV junkie, watching the terror of death unfold into an Insurrection.

Donald Trump refused to listen to his camp, not even his republican brothers and sisters. Mitch McConnell spoke against former president Donald Trump saying "The president is responsible for the mob assault on the Capital, criminals carrying his banners, flags loyalty to Donald Trump and the only one who could have ended this horrifying experience was Donald Trump, an Insurrection on Capitol Hill" There is evidence that, republican Mitch McConnell speaks with false tongues but still hovers over Democracy.

Republican Kevin McCarthy made a stand against the Insurrection for a hot minute by saying" President bears responsibility for Wednesday attack on congress by the mob rioters, he should have immediately denounced the mob when he saw what was unfolding."

What side of Democracy is Kevin McCarthy voicing when trying to become speaker of the House in 2023? Who has invited the Adam's Family to congress, at the same time meet the demands of election deniers and Trump supporters. The media points out that Majority Taylor Green, has become the rising star and replacement of Morelica Adams hanging out with uncle Fester in the house of representatives, inquiring minds want to know has Capitol Hill become The Adam's family domain? Kevin McCarthy pledging to read the entire constitution to his committees won't help him succeed, because of his dedication and participation that brought him a ring kissing ceremony with Trump, now damaged goods holding power.

Men and women today won't look up to God for their forgiveness but instead entertain a strong negative force that has entered the minds of our societies as a functioning component to destroy everyday living. The strongest adversary you will ever encounter during your life time is Satan and the strengths of demonic behaviors. Satan's main objective once again is to destroy and even kill, using methods, schemes and devices to self-destruct by clogging the human minds with dysfunctional thinking and actions exhibited through negative behaviors.

To clearly understand the motives of Satan we must review his history and purpose for the last time. Satan was not always a negative spirit, in fact Satan arrived through an angel called Lucifer, one of the most beautiful angles known to God, remember Lucifer was holy at one given time, on the right side of God.

Lucifer's beauty transformed into a beast named Satan or the Devil, Lucifer stuck on himself wanted to be more powerful than his creator, caused himself to be thrown out of heaven down to earth by God. Lucifer's exile caused a character change, now known as Satan or the devil. Lucifer known as Satan was ejected by God made Satan angry. Satan looking for ultimate revenge, the destroying of his people".

Satan has brought to the earth confusion even though he knows he cannot defeat God. Satan only has a short time to do his dirty work before he will also be destroyed. Satan becomes the war of confusion among God's people, bringing conspiracy theories, propaganda that promotes misleading information and false trues that changes life into darkness. Satan is prince of darkness of the air, just to remind you air is everywhere. Air is what we breath, therefore Satan and his crew is everywhere in the atmosphere.

Satan has many devices that causes disruptions in building your lifestyle, his function is always to destroy, casting the devil out of heaven had an emotional effect on Satan. Satan has conquered many individuals for his army of deceit, so don't be deceived by the devil, written in Rev 12:9 " And the Great Dragon was cast out that old serpent, called the devil and Satan which deceived the earth, and his angels were cast out with him."

Satan tries to cripple your soul causing hate, inductiveness and evil against one's self and others. Satan actually knows God's agenda and his final conquest, Satan has speeded up his mission to act out on a dying world about to self-destruct.

Satan builds his platforms on lies to defeat human existence. Christians must continue to spread the truth and the gospel all over the world, baptizing in the name of Jesus Christ as it is written and take on Peter's advice in I Peters 5:8 "Be sober, be vigilant; because your adversary the "Devil" as a roaring lion, walketh about seeking whom he may devour"

Satan's biggest adversary is working his mental devices, witnessed in daily living, he filtrates his work through our frustrations, stresses and anxieties. Satan works against problem solving and the ability to cognitively think needed in one's life. The danger sets in when anxieties turns into mental disorders, a dysfunction of the mind causing the body to react into physical sickness or physical disorders.

Mental infirmities such as fear, burdens, stresses and anxiety take the road to post-stress-traumatic-disorders. Overwhelmed with poor living condition for self and family with no hope in sight. The mind is full with negative thoughts with no escape to think your way through. But only if you knew Jesus your mind would be free and your Paraclete would be with you.

People in the world working with Satan, who holds the power to sin against God's moral order both natural and spiritual thinking. Has men and women's actions turned into reckless behavior against humanity? What will be the immediate actions of men and women when relief finally come? Will the heart beats of men and women pump for life again? Will life come back again among the American people whose energy for life is almost gone?

There is a conclusion to corrective thinking and behavior by positioning yourself in the right lane of good not evil. A prime example of how God addressed good and evil is found in the book of Genesis. The tree of knowledge of good and evil located in the garden of Eden where it was first established, but not a part of God's decision to activate its purpose. Adam and Eve was tested and ate of the forbidden fruit which opened the door to the knowledge of good and evil, which made men and women today responsible for consequences of their evil actions among all generations up until this very day.

The symbolic reflection of the tree of knowledge of good and evil reveals the choices men and women have to make to commit themselves in achieving correct behavioral actions of good against evil. The knowledge of good and evil pathway is choosing right from wrong through the navigation of society's law and biblical scriptures. America and around the world are at war between good and evil. Former republican congressman Denver Rigg Leman speaks out on June 3 2021, that the war is between good and evil on America's soil.

Prime example on Capitol hill between good and evil tells us this. The republicans blocked a bill for Veterans to treat toxic wombs to get back at the Democrats. What are the important facts? Veterans have been experiencing and exposed to burning pits that causes cancer. This action was supported by our famous republican Senator Ted Cruz demonstrating bumping fist with another republican in voting down the bill, in other words there is no love in the club for our brave Veteran defenders for Democracy.

Republicans has stood by and have done very little, while the Democrats take the heat of today's 2022 crisis in America. Republicans choosing party over country. Takes no stand for Democracy, but to stay loyal to their base while helping themselves to money or political gain, it's a sad day in America, where the war is a fight between good or evil. Satan is creeping into the decisions making process for the American people. No one is asking help from God on these important issues that would reflect humanity.

The things today's politicians are doing against our Democracy is an abomination against God noted in Proverbs 6:16 "Naughty eyes, lying tongues, hands that shed blood, a heart that devises wicked schemes, feet that are swift in running into mischief, false witness who utter lies, spread strife among others" America has witness these actions from politicians, who support party over country, the Republican Reds. A better way of describing the condition of the republicans is said by former republican Riggleman the "crazies is one scoop short of a sundae"

Nevertheless, no human being should demonstrate negative aggressive behavior, instead have an attitude of love as one loves his mother, father, family, relationships and friendships. Men or women may often cry after someone for days, but has never dropped one tear for Jesus who payed with his life for all to be free.

The messages of accountability with God will be an individual thing, responsibility lies with his or her own cross whether it's good or evil, especially leaders after their own lust noted in James 1:14 "But every man is tempted, when he is drawn away of his own lust, and enticed" The price for greed and mistreatment against humanity has to be payed by individuals who assume leadership roles, and commit wrongful acts, the price with God is extremely high and may cost one's life.

A prime example of backlash leadership is following in Trumps parade by Kevin McCarthy, who ran the white house on the shirt tails of Donald trump controlling authority over the republicans, messaging to the republican groupies, who followed Kevin McCarthy's band "do as I say and sign the dotted line, no questions asked, it party over country in the hands of Kevin McCarthy."

Power was lossed by the republican party with Donald Trump's and Kevin McCarthy's plans, the fumes of Donald Trump is still in the air of congress, but with Donald Trump's bad ratings, removed the noose off the necks of some republicans, giving them a chance to denounce warden Kevin McCarthy by blocking him from becoming speaker of the house, a "reap what you sow moment."

Leaders like Kevin McCarthy who has sold himself to the devil, caused men to go astray and not support his efforts, noted in Isaiah 9:26 "For the leaders of this people cause them to err; and they that are led of them are destroyed. Through Kevin McCarthy's challenges he became speaker of the house of representative for 2023, bringing along the Adam's family, but hope is still in the air. Light still shines for America's Democracy, represented by the demo crated party leading the way, senator Hakeem Jefferies a "bipartisanship player" in the land of Democracy.

Prime examples of unpresidential leaders in authority caused the Insurrection on Capitol Hill in Washington D.C January 6, 2021 on America's Democracy. Whether Americans admit the occurrence of the Insurrection or not, there will be a price for violent obstruction against other people. No one is above the law in God's eyes, if you break his law there is no favoritism for anyone but judgement, man's law works according to who you know and how deep your pockets are. Your human rights are with God, always remember people need to thrust after God as one loves his mother, father, family, relationships and friendships.

The reset button for America's corrective behavior seemed so far away, during Trump's administration, the American people fought a Lion and a Bear (Trump and the Republican Reds) like David and Goliath in Biblical history. The commander and chief's purpose seemed to shut down America by defunding the very institutions that has developed mankind's strong hold on America's democratic society. Former president Trump is now in the shadows, left exhibiting neurotic behaviors in calling to throw out the constitution.

America had a reality check during these dark moments when opening Pandora's box. America experienced horrible periods during the Pandemic, but now we must give thanks to a forgotten God. Listening to songs helps us to brings America back with melody from Pattie Labelle. Queen Latifa, and Brandy couldn't sing the words any better "Lord thank you for loving me. Lord thank you for giving me, your grace and your mercy, through my darkest days, all I can say is **"Thank You."**

America needs to say" Thank you" God for relieving America from its worst nightmares during the Pandemic. Calamity after another, yet America prevailed to get the enemy out of America's camp, trusting in the Lord, who is our shepherd to help rebuild what has been destroyed.

The dark clouds that hangs over American skies is only temporary, America has room to blossom again, like the Primrose flower blossoms in the darkness of the night. **Faith**, truth and courage is a good combination to bring light back into America's blooms.

In order to make change in America, **faith** has to become a vision and be restored in the American Dream, including making a better arrangement with God, putting ourselves in the equation of God's living word and actually using what God has provided for you. Noted in Romans 10:17 "So **faith** cometh by hearing and listening by the gospels of "Truth."

Our battle scars maybe deep but we must nonviolently trumpet to the mountain top, bringing our tool box of natural and spiritual knowledge, to assure victory. As Spike Lee says" We most work towards the front door no longer sitting in the back of the bus" always remember **faith** changes things.

Faithfulness must be placed under one's umbrella called "Worship." Worship puts God theology into practice which turns into application through belief and commitment. Noted in Hebrews 11:6 "But without **faith** it is impossible to please him; for he that cometh to God must believe that he is a rewarder of them, that diligently seek hm." **Faith** alone is not the only answer noted in James 2:17 "Even so **Faith,** if it hath not works, is dead being alone your works to bare good fruit is the pleasing of God".

God's universal expectation is to find his Holy people and punish the ones who have oppressed them. The evidence is stated in (Nahum: 1:7): God is jealous and the Lord revenged; the Lord revenged, and is furious; the Lord will take vengeance on his adversaries, and he reserved wrath for his enemies"

To restore your life your **faith** has to have a better arrangement with God, putting all your equations in his hands. Noted in ll Corinthians 5:17 "Therefore if a man be in Christ, he is a new creature; old things are passed away; behold, all things are become new." This is where your "New Day" begins to redirect your steps and open up the way to say "Our Father" who sets us up right for all things. We may not know our directions but through God we are set up right. Believing in our **faith** will carry us through, we now have security in our lives. We have to depend on God to strengthen where weakness is found. Noted in Psalms 138:3 "In the day when I cried thou answered me and strengthen me, and strengthen me with the strength in my soul"

Always remember strong **faith** demonstrates being a great believer, A great biblical example of **faith** is shown by the Children of Israel noted in Hebrews 11:29 "By **faith** they passed through the Red sea on dry land and the Egyptians ordered to bring the Children of Israel back to slavery were drowned. "by **faith** God protected his people".

A herald of changes is needed for Americans to take back responsibility in rebuilding and exercising spirituality. It is important to activate spirituality as a movement for change. American people already use language to represent spirituality without spirituality engagement, people will commit to only using jesters such as Lord, I Hope and pray, Lord please help me, oh my God, please help me Lord and "Jesus "just to name a few.

What is wrong with living Holy? why does it have such a bad

sigma? Yes, there is a sacrifice to live by God's theology but the rewards are plentiful. Why is it such a problem to treat each other right to create solid unity among brotherhood and sisterhood? Our names should represent brothers and sisters instead of democrats, republicans, and independents, the compass that does not work for the American people anymore.

The growth of power among people have blinded their way to using short cut measures such as stems, cheating, manipulation, quick fixes and con games, simply riding on the backs of others to stay powerful.

America's major challenge will be to recreate and maintain a corrective spirit to navigate a rightful life. There are two types of spirits involved, a negative or a positive spirit. Unless your spirit is in the right orbit, the messages written will not be a benefit of guidance in building a better wholesome life style.

Men and women should recognize the almighty God, who gave breath to all from the very beginning of creation, our spirits should give us a reflection of self-worth, God like qualities of intellect, a sense of emotions, passion and creativity.

Your spirit determines your degree of character, your spirit should represent your character to reflect kindness, humbleness strength, skillfulness, knowledge, truth and honesty. A good spirit does not expect a payday for its good works, holy people know where their rewards comes from.

In moving forward, you must separate yourself from any spirits that host ungodly acts. In the book of Proverbs says" in the highways of the upright is to depart from evil, he that kept his way preserved the soul, this message helps shape character for normal living. "There is no room in the club for Satan and the Christian membership is closed concerning the devil and the waiting list is forever. The doors should remain shut tight to your house with no entry, concerning the devil's activities, especially when the devil tries to come between you and God"

Americans must focus on reality to reset in building healthier lifestyles and stop depending on others to direct your path. America has to revisit their history and their relationship with God. According to the Gallup study indicates that 87% Americans say they believe in God. This is a high calculating percentage rate of people believing in God. Image what type of country we would be, if we practiced that percentage in what we preach.

What is the final focus on positioning yourself to build back better in your life as the smoke clears in America for the American people? American people must develop a plan to build a better future and their hearts fixated on healthy lifestyles.

We must trust the very scriptures written to guide us through healthy living. We must carry the blood stain banner given to us by Christians before us to assure God's word will live on. The very scriptures that will help us fight our battles, remove our regrets, tame our burdens and put out the fire of our enemies.

The importance of scriptures brings prophesy, which gives you true understanding of the events you may face or experience in life. The scriptures are instruments for guidance, therefore we must put the very instrument back in our lives taken away from Americans through falsehoods.

It is very important your reading covers Genesis and Revelations to understand the will of God, from the beginning to the end. In the meantime, it is also important to know God's purpose, promise for healthy living. Scripture reading is very important, now the boss in the room for navigating one's life.

The truth lies in this 2,700-year-old best seller that brings God's true prophesy. At the end of this historical journey according to Revelations plainly states in time there will be an end to the madness over the universe.

Bible scriptures encourages you to use God's chosen writers to rely powerful messages such as Paul, noted in (Philippians 3:13) "Brethren I count not myself to have comprehended, but this one thing" I do; forgetting those things which are behind and reaching forth unto those things which are before" You cannot change yesterday but you can improve your tomorrow.

When you become a reader of scripture messaging, it will enlighten your heart noted in Psalms 139: 14 "I will praise thee for am fearfully and wonderfully made; marvelous are thy words; once that my soul knoweth right well." The book of Psalms is a perfect book for reading, it gives you a holistic approach about worship, teaching, encouragement, correction, guidance, emotions, fears, concerns, love and solutions.

Reading the gospels helps explains clearly how and why Jesus was represented as a natural man walking the earth. The reading experience helps men and women better understand the natural existence of Jesus. God gave us a Messiah to lead his purpose and to deliver his message. The time has come for God's sovereignty, knowing the truth about your life and the purpose of its existence.

A woman of Biblical wisdom, blinded in sight but mighty in loving God, testifies that God being a supreme power with authority of the universe, as people we must recognize the heavenly Father who sent his messages through Jesus Christ with a spiritual formula; repent, be baptized and strengthen the mind with the living word, a total surrender to God's sovereignty lies in your hands. Carlene Milledge blinded in sight, strongly puts in conversation that "prayer is the tool for change and anything we seek in life should be through prayer."

God's sovereignty through Jesus Christ addressed reform and to spread the gospel to know who the real creator is. When Jesus walked the earth his teaching and magnificent miracles seemed unbelievable. Jesus's resurrection was on his head, the Roman people and others hated Jesus, hatred ghosted Jesus by crucifixion, but Jesus still rose from the dead, now changed as a spirit, connecting that same spirt to live in everyone. Jesus died on the cross and our sins were pay and every year we celebrate Easter around the world because we know Jesus had an existence.

We must never ignore the price Jesus payed on the cross, every ransom was paid for the sinner to be given his freedom to live freely. Now that we are free, we must fill our minds with the scriptures to build the life Jesus died on the cross for all.

What God needs to know about you, he already knows from your mother's womb. God is a predictor and his predictions come from the living word. God is an analyst, he has already sized up the things in your life, because God controls the time we live in. God doesn't lie, he is dependable.

Psalms 95: 3 For the Lord is a great God and a great King above all Gods therefore there is no one who can measure up to God, the world was created by God and belongs to him. God gives you an indication in Psalms 24:1 "The earth is the Lord and the fullness thereof: the world, and they that dwell therein". Everyone in the world is given an opportunity during their time given, to be a part of this gracious kingdom, but from the past to the present has shown, God's people will try to build their own kingdom without God.

God is preparing for a people to share his kingdom noted in Rev: 21:1 "And I saw a new heaven and a new earth: for the first heaven and the first earth were passed away; and there will be no more sea" God will bring the "Holy City" The new Jerusalem down from heaven for his people, what a day that will be for us to see, if we only believe. The preparation for that day is worth living in our present stay on earth. Psalms 145:13 "Thy Kingdom is an everlasting Kingdom and the dominions endured thought all generations." The scriptures always speak in truth therefore we have to practice living in the truth.

Fixing our hearts towards learning to know God, helps us with our dilemmas, recognizing our weaknesses and turning life into a strong hold to better living. Always work to function at your best in your worst situations and restore and repair along life's journey. Noted in Ephesian 2:10 "For we are his workmanship, created in Christ Jesus unto good works, which God hath before ordained that we should walk in them." You have to work the good in you with obedience, holiness and grace, which will heighten your spirit causing you to fellowship and serve better towards your community.

Knowing God is always a plus no matter the circumstances, your confidence must be developed and built to trust God with all your heart. The most important factor is learning how to listen and pay attention in your surroundings. Listening must become a part of your skill set for better decision making in building a better lifestyle.

Listening to the word will teach you how to humanize your life naturally making good decisions along the way. Noted in Psalms 143:10 "Teach me to do thy will, for thou, art my God; thy spirit is good, lead me into the land of righteousness.

In memory of Larry King a well-respected journalist with a voice, lived by important tools needed to succeed, recommending to his audience that we must position ourselves not to let fear become a road block, but instead drill down with "questioning, listening and learning.

Fear plays a major role in one's life, when we don't know God, one must not let fear stop you from understanding and developing a relationship to know who God really is noted in ll Timothy 1:7 "For God hath not given us the spirit of fear; but of power, and love and of a sound heart" The only thing you should fear is his power towards unrighteous acts and behaviors towards one another. There is a pay day from God for wrong doing, just like it's a payday for wrong doing in society governed by laws.

God's fear should be embraced and looked at in full content, the word fear in most societies, is an emotion that produces being afraid or frighten. If fear is internalized the wrong way, it becomes a spirit of manipulation against self-causing weakness, doubt, immobilized and paralyzed thinking for proper behavioral operations in your life.

In Biblical terms fear represents a symbol to respect God, who is the most powerful source in the universe. Biblical writers view fear as a tool for guidance of God's theology. At the same time God's uses fear as a warning, corrections or judgement tool to keep our lives balanced in a changing world.

Fear is a device used by God for his people against adversaries and entities who are working against his people, therefore consequences will come from God. When you alien yourself up with God, all provisions are taken care of, noted in Psalms 34:9 "O fear the Lord his saints for there is no want to them that fear him," in other words all your mental and physical needs, plus your provisions will be protected by God. You can take this message to the bank.

When God feels his people has compassed him by not listening, noted in Psalms 117:10 "All nations compassed me about; but in the name of the Lord will I destroy them" men and women behaviors today brings this message to life.

One of the biggest obstacles created among men and women is not utilizing their **faith** to communicate with God. Sometimes when walking with God, you may not understand his motives, his decisions, his reasoning, and your pain for believing. The trust in believing comes from your **faith,** the more **faith** the deeper the relationship the stronger the actions in your favor from God.

When we are troubled we must ask God for mercy, because he is merciful noted in Psalms 136 "O Give thanks unto the Lord. for he is good, for his mercy endured forever a life time guaranteed of protection and security.

America is on God's clock for time, while time is ticking away so is the Bible scriptures revealing progressive steps for the final showdown. God will take his throne from man and righteously govern his holy ones, where the final climax will end men and women's control of the universe, oh what a great day to come. Until that day we must walk a Christian life and be examples of conquers in perilous times, at the same time representing America in a holy walk.

Changing your life to a "New Day" brings **faith**, determination and commitment. Your accomplishments will not occur over night, there is a timeline involved. It is important that you include many skills, like time management to assist with scheduling your time daily, monthly and yearly this allows you to measure your growth and foresee changes.

America needs to unify and harmonize with one another, revised the harmony with good character and hearts that shows up at home, workforce, worship, and social interactions. This attitude should be exhibited in your walk and everywhere you go because harmony reflects unity.

A new transition in your life is necessary to stabilize a new norm, the family strength will play an extortionary part, but expect family strength to be tested. Families are prime support systems in building foundations needed, always remember life skills starts or begins at home.

True messaging gives you enough new information needed to re-think with a clear understanding of what God's participation must include. To also know what role God plays in helping you create new visions and healthy living.

Having an open mind gives you an edge to allow information to flow to empower yourself and create self-alliance. Patience, discipline and application are also important factors. Everything you do will be centered around knowledge. Knowledge is a concrete institution navigated through correct fact base findings, research, investigations, with avenues centered around problem solving and solutions.

A trail of fact-based knowledge leads you to critical thinking and good decision making. Knowledge makes you champion over your life and others, when strictly focusing on holistic healthier living. The values of one's knowledge is important to hold on to note in Proverbs 20:15 "There is gold and a multitude of rubies; but the lips of knowledge are a precious jewel.

Knowledge sparks personality improvement, an important tool to add towards building good character, a center that creates intellect. Building character helps you to establish strong holds in trust and honesty recognized by others, demonstrating respect that makes you stand tall, resilience to have courage to bounce back from unfavorable occurrences and pride to stand strong in what you believe is right which reflects humanity.

The focus for change is centered around acknowledging the two types of functioning spirits in the universe. The two spirits are identified as a negative or a positive spirit which exist in humans all over the world. Unless your spirit is in the right orbit, messages read will not be a benefit of guidance in building a better wholesome life style.

In order to move forward you must separate yourself from spirits that host ungodly acts. In the book of Proverbs says" in the highways of the upright is to depart from evil, he that kept his way preserved the soul, this message helps shape character for normal living. The bottom line your spirit must line up with natural and spiritual harmony to be effective in one's life.

Americans must own up too many realities, remove false trues and reset building truthful means to direct your path. One must revisit their past history and their relationship with God. America must return to the ways of truth and put away the lying demons that will trouble your steps in life. Noted in Psalms 119:29 "Remove from me the way of lying and grant me thy law graciously"

What is the final focus in positioning yourself to build back better in your life as the smoke clears in America for the American people? American people must develop a plan to build a better future and having the heart to create healthy lifestyles.

We must trust the very scriptures that was written to guide us through healthy daily living. We must carry the blood stain banner given to us by the Christians before us to assure God's word will live on. The very book that has 31,102 verses that will help us fight our battles, remove our regrets, tame our burdens and put out the fire of our enemies.

Bible scriptures brings prophesy, which gives true understanding of the events you may face or experience in life. The bible scriptures are an instrument for guidance; therefore, we must put this very instrument back in our lives taken away from Americans through falsehoods. The truths lie in this 2,700-year-old best seller that brings God's true prophesy. At the end of this historical journey according to Revelations plainly states in time, there will be an end to the madness over the universe.

Bible scriptures encourages change using God's writers to rely the message from God, such as Paul noted in (Philippians 3:13) "Brethren I count not myself to have comprehended, but this one thing" I do; forgetting those things which are behind and reaching forth unto those things which are before" You cannot change your yesterday, but you can improve your tomorrow.

When you become a reader of the scriptures the message will

enlighten your heart noted in Psalms 139: 14 "I will praise thee for am fearfully and wonderfully made; marvelous are thy words; once that my soul knoweth right well." The book of Psalms is perfect for reading, which gives you a holistic approach about worship, teaching, encouragement, correction, guidance, emotions, fears, concerns, love and solutions.

Reading the four gospels helps you clearly understand Jesus came as a human being, a natural man walking the earth to help us better understand and relate to his word in a natural form. God gave us a Messiah to lead his purpose, Jesus was chosen to deliver this message. The time had come for God's sovereignty knowing the truth about your life and the purpose of its existence.

God being a supreme power with authority of the universe, everyone should recognize the heavenly Father, who sent his messages through Jesus Christ with a spiritual formula; repent, baptize, and strengthen the mind with the living word. A total surrender to God's sovereignty, using this formula will bring the holy spirit upon you to be used as your comforter, anointed power and protector.

God's sovereignty is to produce, reform and spread the living word to reflect, who the real creator is. Jesus being human like ourselves made it easier for families to understand Jesus teaching and magnificent miracles that seemed unbelievable. A ransom was on Jesus's head, so they crucified him on the cross in Galilee.

Jesus was crucified and rose from the dead, he rose as a spirit, to connect the dots for our well-being, the same spirit to live in every one of us. Jesus died on the cross and our sins were pay for and free will given. Every year we celebrate Easter around the world because we know Jesus had an existence.

America can unite with harmony for one another, by revising the love in their hearts that shows up at home, workforce, worship, and social interactions, everywhere we go harmony creates unity.

You have examined true messaging which gives you enough information needed to re-think with a clear understanding of God's participation and what must be included to creating new visions and healthy living. God is a spirit who created men and women under that same spirituality examined in Biblical history.

To begin using this concrete information, it is necessary to do a self-evaluation of where you are mentally and physically fit, this evaluation gives you a picture of what areas you will need to work on to accomplish your goals. The **New Day** challenges will have many tasks and obstacles to overseer. Another important factor is to inventory your skill sets, this helps to determine what tools you have on hand and what tools to acquire in repairing or reconstructing a better direction in building a personal portfolio.

Always remember, the more resources and networks you make available the more empowerment you have in reaching goals. The best environment you can work in is your family structure, people who love you will cheer you on to create great endeavors and be there through thick and thin.

You must understand your purpose as an individual to better create your directions, you cannot be double minded, you must have a clear understanding of who you are. Noted in James 1:8 "A doubled minded man is unstable in all his ways."

Christian life will give you balance to change your walk to reflect representing the truth in love, exercising the body to stay fit in scriptures for daily living. Walking wisely in the light brings good fruit, goodness, and righteousness because your Christian walk is your strength and your reflection to daily living.

Testimonies is the strong hold in your life, it reflects the past struggles and challenges you have overcome by God's grace and now you can say it out loud "This is my testimony that left scars of discomfort in my life but "Oh when I met Jesus my testimony became by rock to stand on for better days ahead". Testimonies demonstrates the renewing of one's **faith** because it shadows those situations God moved in your favor.

With the spirit of Jesus in your soul, requires putting on the whole armor for God, necessary for successful daily living. In Ephesians 6:11 "Put on the full armor of God so that you can stand against the tactics of the Devil" You have to have both feet in with God, a total commitment to battle with any unfair rulers of authority, powers reflecting darkness and negative forces working against you.

Wearing God's whole armor keeps your battles short and successful, as we march and triumph for the freedom of our lives, take back what God gave us to create our healthy living. We must lift up our voices to the highest notes and demand what we dream for.

Leaders who recognize God's gifts becomes ambassadors to harmonize living, promoters of good will and faith, sharing positive energy among others here in America. The time has come for the churches to stand up and go to the battlefield, spreading the word and sharing cornerstones of God's love and peace. According to Bishop Lambert Gates representing Kingdom Apostolic Ministries, speaking out in a great Sunday vertical message, during the Pandemic. Telling his listeners that the saints must come off the church pews and march for justice in an unjust world.

Bishop Lambert Gates Jr. declares his messaging to the church, that we have favor with the Lord and when we pray, our **faith** in God is going to change things. In the meantime, while we wait on the lord our steps must be on the move for the justice of God's people here in America and around the world.

The Christians of the church who love God is also affected by ungodly powers, but we must not be silent. Bishop Lambert Gates continues to spell out important Bible scriptures to support his ministry conveying to his listeners Noted in Isaiah 58:1" Cry aloud spare not, life up thy voice like a trumpet, and show my people their transgression and the house of Jacob their sins."

Together we must triumph over yesterday's mistakes and make honest changes and be careful because bad decisions take years to undo. If you want change, your job is to stand in the right aisles working to harmonizing both the natural and spiritual mind working for progress.

God knows man can drift from the word, there are avenues to keep you on course noted in Proverbs 27:8 "As a bird wondered from his nest; so is a man that wondered from his place." Therefore, just brush yourself off, stand up straight and keep your life moving in the right direction. When God has you covered you will not fall noted in Psalms 94:18 When I said my foot slippeth: thy mercy, Lord held me up"

Always hold dear to your testimonies, a language to victories stories from a person's triumph, overcoming challenges conquered through God's mercy and grace. It's a shared message to give others hope in overcoming their unfavorable experiences and to build a better life.

We can't get caught in the moment after the landsides American experienced, America must take to greater heights, a better tomorrow, reaching the stars only to come back to building a bigger, better America.

Sometimes the way for change in America seemed almost impossible, but in 2021 the people demonstrated a united front in key states, like Georgia, fought back against Trump's gymnastic team to overturn the people's vote for American Democracy and their dreams became a golden kind of a day, a true reality, a united front. In the fight always remember noted in Psalms 144:1 Blessed by the lord my strength, which teaches my hands to war, and my fingers to fight. In life you will have wars to fight sometimes alone and sometimes with others for justice.

The time to fight came upon the horizon of the Georgians once again, In the 2022 Georgia election runoff between Herschel Walker and Senator Warnock. The world was watching the scenes of good vs evil, in the end of the journey God kept his gate-keeper, Senator Warnock, who received 51.1 percentage of the votes to win the Georgia election, having another golden kind of a day and a victory. Senator Warnock victory speech included an important acknowledgement for the world to here " There are four most important words in America "The people have spoken" the end results came in spoken word "There is harmony and power in the people vote"

The importance of living in harmony with others helps you to build back better in a natural and spiritual manner. Both components have to demonstrate love for harmony to produce the results you are

141

looking for in your life. Always remember, as **faith** increases the spiritual overseers the natural being. Your spiritual empowerment is given by God to achieve your highest height here on earth and at the same time buying a double Indemnity life Insurance plan for eternal life.

Living in God's world brings challenges, the earth needs healing, God gives us science to explore and keep the earth at its best. Scientists are provided to cure the ailments of the universe with scientific methods. In 2020 a killing virus, called Covid 19 hit America's soil as a world wind, killing and taking name, with many unknown challenges for cure.

Thanks to the birth of Modena, Pfizer and Johnson vaccine blessed America, God's gave mercy to his people to bare the virus. The cure for any healing takes time and patience, especially the cure for the killer Pandemics American people faced and around the world. All Americans have not yet chosen to help kill the variants of these Pandemics, by simply supporting community efforts, therefore the famine stays on the land to create deadlier viruses such as the Omicron period spreading at the rate of 95% over the Delta.

America is consistently experiencing calamities with stronger variants like the Omicron, BA5 and now the spread of a disease called Monkeypox. American people must be obedient during the era of the Pandemics and the spread of different diseases. American people should know what preventive measures to take, its simple stay vaccinated, continue to social distant, washing hands, mask-up and stay away from things that causes transmitted diseases. Americans must continue to have **faith** and give God the praise for covering our lives while we wait for total relief in the cure of these Pandemic variants and their rapidness in spreading diseases.

Americans must continue to have **faith** and give God the praise for covering our lives while we are given another chance to build back better. If man continues to ignore the signs of God there will be little relief to conquer the aliments of the ongoing variants that has now attack the children of our societies.

The amazing thing about the Bible it's a predictor of what's to come, revealing events people will experience in the days to come. An example people saw happened in 2022. Kentucky catastrophic storms made history, rain producing 4" per hour leaving 14 to 16 inches of flooding and taking lives. Everything that is happening to us right now has been identified in the **Good book scriptures** that so many people ignore. The Bible speaks on all world current events, how does the bible's scriptures documents have such predictions and insight?

The signs of America's challenges to change is still upon the land, the power of God's hand is shown just before the week of Christmas in 2022, a celebration of the holiday for Jesus Christ. A deadly weather wintery experience covered the nation, called "Bomb cyclone" affecting central and eastern United States.

The snow cyclone rapidly moving across the nation, heavy snow and rain brings record-breaking temperatures thrusting at 80% below temperatures, hailing winds taking charge in most states pushing heavy snow around the nation, leaving misery behind, at the same time heavy flooding happening in other parts of the United States, turning roads into rivers.

205 million people across the U.S, experiencing a nightmare just before Christmas day, record breaking flight cancellations and stranded people experiencing life threating deep freeze of coldness paralyzing travel. This type of weather happens once in a generation, winds coming at 50 miles an hour. Man has no power to stop the snow cyclone condition, time and patience is the only hope for relief, the power of weather elements belongs to God. America today should have enough experience in warning signs due to their, corruption, disobedience and the mistreatment of Gods people.

The scriptures speak its prophecy. the time will come when men and women will not know the seasons, where hot seasons turns cold and cold seasons becomes hot, why did this prophecy just happen to the nation? The evidence of judgement is our landmark during the nation's Christmas holiday season.

To answer the unknown events, warrant having insight to various scriptures, self-Bible learning will help you to understand the unthinkable. The bible will lead you to navigate your way in life to avoid false doctrine, wrong persuasion and judgement of people imitating God. Noted in Matt 24:5 For many shall come in my name, saying I am Christ; and shall deceive many" President Donald Trump made a statement saying "I am the chosen one" The need for Trump power goes even deeper when demons have control of a person's mind.

Americans must take responsibility to include God on a daily basis not just making Christmas a prime example of recognition. All over the world the story of baby Jesus is celebrated at Christmas time. Noted in Matthews 1:21 "And she shall bring forth a son, and thou shalt call "JESUS": for he shall save his people from their sins" American celebrates Jesus wonderful birthday with sparkling decorations, cookies and candies, Christmas cards, find foods and lots of presents with love, shared with our families on Christmas day.

The evidence is on the wall, every Christmas, Pope Francis holds Christmas eve mass in St Peter's Basilica followed with a Christmas state address, where thousands attend to get the feeling of Jesus Christ at Christmas time. Thousands of other churches all over the world, have traditions of celebrating the birth of Jesus Christ on Christmas day.

Jesus should never be forgotten no never, we must always carry him in our minds and our hearts, so that we can accomplish great things and make life worthwhile. Bishop Jacklyn McMullen is a diehard for shedding light on a conversation "Lord help my mind". Expressing the importance on how we must embrace the holy spirit to guide us in everyday living. We must first surrender our self-including the mind.

The mind has to be offered up to learning prayer and worship, Ecclesiastic 39:1 "But he that giveth his mind to the law of the highest, and is occupied in the meditation thereof, will seek out wisdom of the ancient, and be occupied in prophecies" It is important to note, filling the mind is a method for "food for thoughts" a way to corrective thinking, remember the mind controls the body.

The mind must pivot in the direction of corrective thinking as you grow into your new day with God's righteousness and purity of truth. In your natural spirit you must rid bittiness, anger, insult, slander and wickiness or wrong doings. Change all negative behavior and habits, replace them with the knowledge of good character building to stand on even ground for yourself and your family.

This change will not happen overnight, but what will happen when being consistent as Sam Cooks sings in his lyrics "There been times that I thought I wouldn't last long, now I think I'm able to carry on, it's been a long time coming, but I know a "**change**" is going to come"

The real challenge for change will be to control your flesh, while building a healthy life style and maintaining a spiritual orbit. The word flesh mentioned in Biblical terms represents and describes the function of your behavior both physically and mentally in a natural setting governed by your flesh. The flesh has no spiritual orbit, it has to be introduced to human spiritual operations.

The Flesh is at war with the spirit of God's theology when dealing with human behavior. The flesh is lovers of pleasure at anyone's cost and may not have limits on their unfavorable behavior such as strife, sex immorality, envy, jealousy, lover of self and inhuman acts, just to name a few. Sin has an attachment to the flesh noted in John 1:21 "If we say we have no sin, we deceive ourselves and the truth is not in us"

In your lifetime you have the ability to live righteous, yearning for the gospels that empowers us, magnifies life, lifts up spirits in the time of trouble, activate our movements to endure our trials and tribulations, which gives a new attitude towards life. Noted in Romans 5:3 "And not only so, but we glory in tribulations also; knowing that tribulations worketh patience.

Once You have accepted Jesus Christ and baptized by the living word you will be anointed with a gift called the **Holy Spirit** in time, all powers needed to guide you, supplied by the holy spirit. Your spirit will be empowered to keep you ahead of your trials and tribulation. The holy spirit will help you endure your situation until change comes, remember the holy spirit is your protector and comforter.

The 10 commandments were written to build God's platform and strengthen his foundation, especially towards conduct and morality. As time moved on, caused changes in God's ordinance for more empowerment of his people towards perfection. God decided to make transformation through Jesus who shredded his blood on the cross which makes him the mediator of the New Testament by means of Jesus's death, a guiding movement involving the holy spirit.

The holy spirit's birth was evolved In the New Testament, God chose the holy spirit to be used as a defense against flesh disobedience and correcting behaviors when necessary. The holy spirit is a spirit inside of you to help individuals to stay on track, and to help maintained a better balance in your life through the holy spirit.

During periods of your life, the holy spirit will bring you necessary tools noted in: Romans 5:4 "And patience, experiences; and experience, hope" and from there God will give you rest " Now you are in a paraclete covering for personal guidance that brighten your morning star, you are safe in the heart of God, who loves you.

The holy spirit gives you the spirit to forgive and expose unquestionable truth which helps you empower yourself to walk-in truth, the holy spirit helps you balance life with love and peace.

The holy spirit is not a magical spirit or attached to witchcraft, this power is strictly given by God. The holy spirit holds its own and covers its own territory, standing alone in power. Paraclete (holy spirit} an advocate, representation of Christ. A companion that walks beside you, promise never to leave you, to help you in areas of doubt, unbelief, envy, jealousy and mis- trust.

The holy spirit helps to inspires our hearts to feel that God is beside you, morally and spiritually. The holy spirit helps us when we are overwhelmed, a guiding light, it's your side kick you never had.

God's paraclete is your benefactor, it works with your infirmities, weaknesses, and helps you not to become slave to the flesh, it's your companion, partner in everything you do and to inspire your heart.

The holy spirit balances your steps and control the flesh that has tasted sin, the more pleasures of sin the harder it is to live righteously.

Holy Christians position warrants sacrifice, let God dwell in your hearts through **faith.** Plant a seed for yourself where your roots will grow in love. Walk worthy of your calling you have received from God with humility, gentleness, patience and keeping the unity of the spirit with peace.

A Christian's job is to build up the body of Christ with God's doctrine of one body, one spirit, one lord, one faith, one baptism, and knowing there is only one God above all.

The tools for Christians are building from the Holy scriptures (Bible), which helps maintain your position to avoid being surrounded by incorrect teaching, empty doctrines, cunning movements, clever techniques of deceitful, propaganda and setting your mind up in mazes you'll never get out of.

Renewing the mind is a never-ending cycle because time is always changing things. Keeping alert using the scriptures for all circumstances because your guidance is written in the scriptures. No matter the time or era, whatever circumstances occurs in your life, the Bible is equipped to assist you.

Complete clarity of your purpose and acceptance of God's grace will gain accuracy, and literacy to walk your Christian life, shouting to the world "I am blessed by God's grace and his mercy".

Biblical writers like Joshua, God noted in Joshua 1.9 "Have I not commanded you? Be strong, courageous, do not be frightened, do not be dismayed, for the lord your God is everywhere you go" Now you can't beat that security, because as we walk in this natural life we have to pray for the seen and unseen dangers in our lives and this is the reason we soldier up for God!".

America has fallen but not out, we have been saved by grace, therefore America can't get caught in the moment after the landsides American experienced, America must take to greater heights, a better tomorrow, reaching the stars only to come back to building a bigger, better America

Dark moments can't represent the people in America, we are God's people created to triumph over darkness to bring light to the front row. President Biden made a promise and made good on his promise to get the American people back their Democracy, a demonstration of righteous people proving the power to change things lies in the people's vote. The Maga-Republicans stood dormant not to improve the American dream, trying to make president Biden fail his mission.

The Dark moment of America's experience cannot be blamed just on the republican representatives, working on the wrong side of the block, remember people voted to supported the madness, because they also occupy that same block with no harmony in site.

The importance of living in harmony with others helps you to build back better in a natural and spiritual manner. Both components need love to harmonize with one another to produce the results you are looking for in your life. Always remember, as your **faith** increases the spiritual being increases the authority over your natural being, your spiritual empowerment is given by God to achieve your highest height on earth and at the same time buy a double indemnity life Insurance plan for eternal life.

There is more to life than just striving for richness when achieving your goal, why gain all the richness in life and lose you humanity and favor with God. Living greedy without sharing brings about suffering, preventing the enjoyment of your wealthy lifestyle.

When the mind is set for learning how to pray and worship with the highest, than the soul will be feed with the right nutrition. Noted in Romans12:2 "Do not conform to the patterns of the world but transformed by the renewing of the mind, then you will be able to test and approve what God's will is, his good pleasing and perfect will."

When the mind's function is right, the spirit of a person's performance reflects his or her movement in life. A rightful spirit sees through the lens of spiritual kindness and rightful living. In all that had been written or said about harmonizing your life, it's your spirit that leads the way. If the spirit isn't right there is nothing to make you a champion over one's life, having no room for advancement.

Charity is an action of spiritual kindness, charity out ranks faith and hope according to the Bible in Corinthians 13:13 "And now abide faith, hope and charity, but the greatest of these is charity" Charity should be included in your spirit because your spirit never dies whether the spirit is good or bad, it is your spirit that determines your character to reflect kindness, humbleness, strength, giving, honesty, trust and righteousness. The spirit is the real deal, it reflects how you operate your life that affects others in family, friendship, employment and relationships.

During your lifetime you have the ability to live righteous, yearning for the gospels that empowers you, magnifies life and lifts up your spirits in the time of trouble. Activate our movements to endure trials and tribulations and gives a new attitude towards life. Noted in Romans 5:3 "And not only so, but we glory in tribulations also; knowing that tribulations worketh patience.

There are examples on how we maintain our righteousness through messages both from natural and holy living. Humans will always need sound knowledge to survive for recognizing the power of both natural and spiritual waters which is a part of human existence, God allows water to be a part of life's necessity, the living water in the scriptures is described as a symbolic characteristic, spiritual living waters means having a secure and meaningful life with God.

Water in our daily living is very important because without the availability of water, the body could not survive. Water in the spiritual representation offered by God as a symbol of righteousness living. Noted in John 7:38 "He that believeth on me, as the scriptures hath said, out of his belly shall flow rivers of living water." If you stand for righteousness God promises you will never thirst for anything, meaning there is nothing to thrust for, because the soul will be satisfied and taken care of by God.

All the pathways to knowledge bring you truth for successfully governing your life and activate a stronger destiny. In order to change the world, you must be true to your natural living with a spiritual orbit. When you really love God, it will reflect in your behavior. If you have no solution to life, then your life will be subject to evil, revenge and hate with no fuel for a new life of opportunity.

Prayer and worship are the key to an intimate relationship to achieve a better relationship with God, he works out the good in us, preparing and fixing our hearts, working out your dilemmas, turning weakness into a strong hold which brings restoration. God gives you a platform to work out the good in you, to become more obedient, fellowship and service and most importantly, demonstrating the beauty of holiness with the Father the creator.

We might not know our destiny to the future, but when you walk with God you are automatically set up right, to meet any challenge and your **faith** will carry you through. You become secure, covered, sealed and anchored by God and his living word, therefore our **faith** will not shift and our lives become harmonized. Your security has been set up right by God to keep your righteous ways and secure your relationship with God.

Patience is also needed for change, but we also know patience can be uncomfortable, at certain times there may be a waiting period to accomplish your goal, but remember being preserved leads to solutions. Noted in Psalms 34:15 "The eyes of the lord are up on the righteous, and his ears are open unto their cry" just know God got your back, keep praying and be patience for what you are asking for.

Noted in Philippians 4:6 "Do not be anxious about anything, but in everything by prayer and petition, with thanksgiving, present your request to God" The message for what you need in life is self-explained, if you **believe.** Always remember you can talk to God anytime you feel like it, when other may not have the time for you.

Preserve your heart to position itself not to be contaminated or polluted with false trues and actions of unrighteousness behavior, but the glory of God the creator to shine his beauty into your heart. Keeping the heart filled with emotional and spiritual feelings to express your walk with God, pressing your way to stay a celebrity in the mix of God's theology leaving your prints in the sand of righteousness during your life time. Always remember God's judgement is from the participation of the heart to do good will. Stay centered, fixed, setup and established with the living word to help equip you for better healthy living.

Let's us not forget the power of grace, where your helps come from and receiving grace through **faith** is an acceptance of righteousness, for when you walk in grace with God you can conquer what is needed for healthy living. Grace is your mercy, forgiveness, tender kindness, and your help, a complete insurance policy with God.

Life with Christ is like a palm tree always growing year after year under all types of circumstances, reaching higher and higher in faith. The palm tree is a righteous symbolic meaning demonstrating unbreakable strength in a person's life, not like the grass used as a symbol that wants to stand among the strong but takes the short cut to life, that grows quickly. If grass become exposed to extreme circumstances like hot weather condition, the grass will wither burn and die. Always remember some people flourish quickly but their success does not last, but burns and dies.

The palm tree can live forever even in the desert, withstanding extreme weather conditions, where their leaves never dry up, fall off or change colors they always remain green. The palm tree lives for hundreds of years, as the palm tree ages, it still continues to bear fruit. Life will flourish with prosperity when you demonstrate loyalty in keeping a faithful relationship with God noted in Psalms 92:12 The righteous shall flourish like a" Palm tree"

Today's women are symbols like the palm tree mentioned, standing strong as they want to be. Time has come for women to be acknowledged in handling many more responsible and respectable roles, just not having the roles of daughters, sisters, mothers and wives.

In the eyes of some spiritual leaders mentions that the bible speaks, a woman should be silent and take on no leadership's roles especially over the man. There are scriptures in the Bible that mentions women's roles, that has to be viewed carefully. When God calls a person for his purpose, he decides whether it will be a man or woman for the Job.

God demonstrated his choice in the book of Judges where the Israelites again did evil, where the Lord sold them into the hands of King Jubin, who had the Israelites enslaved for 20 years. God chose

Deborah a great woman prophetess of wisdom, revelations, and discernment to be judge of Israel. In Biblical history God chose a woman to Judge, orchestrate and help the Israelites problem solving their welfares.

With a large Army of 10,000 warriors, God guided Deborah to victory, noted in Judges 4:9 " And she said, I will surely go with thee: notwithstanding the journey that thou takest shall not be for thine honor; for the Lord shall sell Sisera into the hand of a woman." Deborah's leadership skills, prevailed against King Jubin of Canaan and brought back peace for the kingdom that reigned for 40 years.

A woman's blue print is now in the sands of America's dream, her courage today will take leadership roles in helping America maintain greatness. Always remember out of the rib of Adam came a gift to the world, a woman named Eve, who performed a great miracle in the world "The **reproduction of mankind**." In our natural eyes we see her as magical, in our spiritual eyes we see her as a miracle.

Women are the spring board of family structure, her faith is strong in embracing commitment in the fight for moving the American dream forward, looking for no recognition in her stride. Women are the CEO's for the operation of their children and family, the Joana Ark when trouble appears, swinging her mighty sword for humanity.

Faith accommodates women of the world, their strength in love, courage, resilience, commitment and caretaking for humanity. God has always place women in positions at the right time to carry the cross for herself and others. In Psalms 46:5 is written "God is in the midst of her; she shall not be moved; God shall help and that right early" A Salute to all mothers and women, all over the world who are silent with their contributions and have made the difference."

The important note to remember in this entire reading is to clearly understand how life unfolds with your purpose in mind, to give you a direction of natural living that orbits around spirituality. The task will be to renew the mind entirely and become a new creation under God's command, learning not to conform to the patterns of the world, but be tested and approved of what God's free will is all about. What you must do is noted in Colossians 3:2 "Set your minds on things above, not on earthy things, preparation for external life has to be done here on earth".

A very important commandment most people do not know about is baptism, noted in Act 2:47 " Can any man forbid water that these should not be baptized which have received the Holy Ghost" In biblical history God demanded baptism Noted in Acts 2:48 "And he commanded them to be baptized in the name of the Lord. You must be baptized as you first step into your new day in walking with God. Baptism is symbolic, it represents death, burial and resurrection of Jesus Christ and can only be accepted through immersion of water.

There is no ransom for your sins with God except repentance, a word spoken to say "Sorry for my sins." Following in the footsteps of what Peter noted in (Acts 2:38) "Repent and be baptized." Evangelist VonCiele Dukes expressing in spoken words in an evening service "Altar call" asking an important question to the congregation, "How can I be saved?" The word repentance came to mind and at the same time, Evangelist Dukes message flowed into the congregation of the saints, who often say "God is good " and with her last words, she shouted to the audience saying **"VonCiele is saying "'God is so good."** In sister Evangelist Dukes messaging plainly says **"Don't miss out on what God has in stored for you because of the lack of baptism!**

If you let people take your God away, you will have nothing to depend on to be your guiding light, if there is no light, strife can be a constant enemy because happiness comes and goes, but joy always comes back as the scripture noted in Psalms 30:5 "Weeping may endure for a night; but joy cometh in the morning"

When the sun does not shine in your life at the moment, be your strongest and believe noted in Proverbs 3:4-5 "Trust in the LORD with all thine heart; and lean not unto thine own understanding" (5) In all thy knowledge him; and he shall **direct thy past**."

"The bible scriptures are the messenger for the last days of the world existence under man, it is your navigator to holiness which calls for change. Many people carry their bibles when they attend church but never have really read it, or even concern in what's in it.

When people carry their bibles, it seems to makes them think they are in the right lane of life, but one must note, every man and woman will be responsible for God's doctrine and carrying their own cross and the consequences behind it, because it is written in the scriptures.

We must follow the doctrine that God set before us noted in Deuteronomy 32:21 "My doctrine shall drop as the rain, my speech shall distill as the dew, as the small rain upon the tender herb. and as the showers upon the grass" Jesus is our rock to stand upon Noted in Deuteronomy 32:4 "He is the rock, his work is perfect; for all his ways are judgement; a God of truth and without iniquity, just and right is he."

Commandments has been set before us, which most people are familiar with, but there are other commandments hardly spoken but a demand from God, Noted in John 15:12 "This is my commandment that ye love one another as I have loved you." God created love as one of the strongest emotions a person owns. Loves is a penetrating feeling most people have experienced, Jesus clearly tell us noted in John 15:9 "As the father has loved me, so have I loved you, continue ye in love" As humanitarians we must spread the love.

A faithful composer follows his imagination and creates his life from his soul that makes life come alive. A new spirit on your journey will be on the highway of holy living evolving around patterns of compassion, kindness, humility, gentleness, and love, because God is love. Noted in Rev.22:14 "Blessed are they that do his commandments that they may have the right to the tree of life and may enter in through the gates of the city"

We stand up for what we have the courage for, demand what we have invested in our natural and spiritual life. Petition God for what we need through prayer noted in St Luke 11:9 "And I say unto you ask and it shall be given, you seek and ye shall find; knock, and it shall be opened unto you." also noted in verse 10"For everyone that asked, receiveth and he that seek findth, and to him that knocked it shall be opened. This is a **promise** given by God if you only believe!

The American people have to rely on their **faith** because **faith** comes with freedom of endurance to keep coming towards God until you have conquered your conquest. **Faith** can conquer hopelessness and move towards trumpet, persistence to make right decisions for rightful living. Knowing to press your way with all your handicaps until you receive the power to remove all unhealthy situations. Be determine to be different and the desire to make change, **faith** moves mountains.

Spiritual living represents God's divine order as you walk with God, some of the most important factors comes from the scriptures to guide you to application. The messages you have learned through scriptures should create successful daily living.

A powerful tool in changing for a better living is patience, noted in Hebrews 10:36 "For you have need of patience, that after ye have done the will of God ye might receive the **promise.**

End messages are the best to remember, we must acquire unbreakable **faith** needed to build a lifestyle of choice. **Faith** walking is a representation in believing in your specialties like Mahalia Jackson's traveling all over the world letting people know, the love of God in her voice with a melody in her heart. Mahalia Jackson knew she was a child of the highest, her style brought out the best in a person with the clapping of the hands and the tapping of your feet, knowing in song there is a mighty God.

Mahalia Jackson had a beautiful profile of beauty and elegance no matter where she traveled, her unbreakable **faith** stayed on the road of glory. During her time, she knew people needed to hear comforting songs, that pieced hearts to hold on to during their struggles in life, knowing that her singing was nourishment for the soul. Mahalia's acknowledgement demonstrates the power of unbreakable **faith** an African American vocalist singing **"How I got over".**

Unbreakable **faith** is a symbol that only the heart can carry, unbreakable **faith** flows in many hearts shining their light on one another, connecting you to this beautiful, wonderful actress, Loretta Devine who stands up in a mighty way for spirituality through performing arts. The over flowing of her wisdom through her performances can make us all laugh and sometime cry, but it's all shared with her audience no matter the territory of acting. Loretta Devine's just a "Phenomenal woman"

Let's not stop expressing the love for God, because the cup is running over. Close your eyes for a moment and go to the musical world for a melody from the lips of someone golden, singing with a voice that enters the depths of the soul, taking you on a journey only **Whitney Houston** can do, expressing the joy we can be confident about, when we trust God " I sing because I am happy, I sing because I am free, his eyes is on the sparrow and I know he watches me. Whitney songs has pierced our hearts for what we need in life through song, giving you just a bit of fresh air when her voice shares the skies with the almighty God.

Whitney knows in song where our helps comes from, she spreads her lyrics calling on heaven to say "Hear me now because her winter storms has darkened her sun, after all, her strength has gone, even her melodies are gone, but she can still hear a song from God," as she sings **"I look to you"** explains it all.

Faith is King messaging can be witnessed through pathways of God's holiness and his expectations of all human beings. The real reality, God is a jealousy God noted in Exodus 34:14 " For thou shall worship no other God but the Lord, whose name is Jealous, he is a jealous God, therefore when you turn against the one who made you, God notes " They have provoked me to anger with their vanities and I will move them to jealousy with those which are not a people; will provoke them to anger with a foolish nation."

A great soldier by the name of Daniel Dukes went to battle for the United States Army in War ll with unbreakable faith. During his mission in Germany as a soldier, carried his unbreakable **faith** in his back pocket, the 23 third Palms on a handkerchief, believing his unbreakable faith with God will carry him through the war and home safely back to America and he was given the **promise.**

Faith has left you will this conversation, a message of strength 23rd Psalms:

"Lord is my Shepard, I shall not want; he marketh me lie down in green pastures; he leadth me besides the still waters, he restoreth my soul; he leadeth me in the path of righteousness for his name sake, thou I walk through the valley of the shadow of death, I will fear no evil; for thou art with me, thy rod and staff they comfort me, Thou preparest a table before me in the presents of my enemies, thy anointest my head with oil; my cup runneth over, surely goodness and mercy shall follow me all the days of my life in the house of the lord forever," this is the badge of honor in the messages of Faith is King.

Standing approved with God's formula, will create strong methods to help you in analyzing your situation for change, organizing your priorities, memorizing your purpose, verbalizing in what you believe in and personalize your relationship with God. Let God know that he is your hero, the wind beneath you wing and the sky is unlimited for what you dream for.

There is a universal message we must all seek Noted in John1:5 "This is the message which we have heard of him, and declare unto you, that God is light in him is no darkness at all"